ALBION W. TOURGÉE

ALBION W. TOURGÉE

BY

ROY F. DIBBLE

KENNIKAT PRESS, INC./PORT WASHINGTON, N. Y.

8/3. 4
T727X
D5-43a

110511

Copyright 1921 by Lemke and Buechner
Reissued in 1968 by Kennikat Press
Library of Congress Catalog Card No: 68- 16287
Manufactured in the United States of America

TO MY FATHER AND MOTHER

PREFACE

In this book I have attempted to weave into a single narrative the various threads of interest in the life of Tourgée, soldier, carpet-bagger, politician, judge, consul, lecturer, editor and publisher, political writer, and novelist. The idea of writing his biography would quite certainly never have occurred to me had I not spent my early years in a cherished rural community, hardly centralized enough to be dignified even by the name of hamlet, only four miles from Thorheim. One of my earliest recollections is of hearing my father say what sounded to me then like a single word, "Judgetorjáy," which very much aroused my childish curiosity. And while engaged in the work of collecting material and of writing, I have often been cheered by the thought that the published results of my researches might afford some pleasure to many friends and acquaintances of mine, who knew Tourgée not so much as a prominent novelist as a genially democratic neighbor. I can only hope that the picture of him which I have drawn (in which task I have been prompted only by the love of impartial, but I trust not unsympathetic, truth) will not cause any of his friends to hold in less esteem the only literary person of importance who has added the lustre of legendary charm to a spot already graciously favored by nature, but will rather enable them to have a juster comprehension of the reasons for their admiration.

PREFACE

Both the demand of prefatory conciseness and the impossibility of expressing in an adequate manner the gratitude I feel toward many persons whose kindly interest has been shown me in multitudinous ways, somewhat disconcert me at this time. To Mrs. Elizabeth S. Warner, now mistress of Thorheim, who placed all of Tourgée's private correspondence, together with masses of unpublished material, at my disposal, and also favored me with a wealth of anecdote and generous hospitality, I owe the greatest debt of all. Professor Carl Van Doren read my manuscript chapter by chapter as it was written and helped me with much penetrating criticism. My thanks are also due to Professors W. P. Trent, A. H. Thorndike and G. P. Krapp, who gave me the benefit of their ripened scholarship. My colleague, Doctor R. F. Jones, read my manuscript with painstaking care. Professor Archibald Henderson, of the University of North Carolina, and Professor C. Alphonso Smith, of the United States Naval Academy, put me in touch with various sources of information. Several of Tourgée's classmates of Rochester University and a number of residents in Greensboro, North Carolina, furnished me with much illustrative material. The recent death of Mrs. Tourgée prevents me from showing her my appreciation for the record of her husband's life which she kept for so many years—a record upon which she would have based her own biography of him, had not the memories of their past experiences aroused in her emotions so poignant that she was unable to put her plan into execution.

Roy F. Dibble.

Columbia University, May, 1920.

CONTENTS

ALBION W. TOURGÉE

CHAPTER I

BIRTH—EDUCATION—THE WAR

"As far as the mere facts of my birth, residence, and occupation are concerned," says Tourgée in a letter dated August, 1894, to a college president who had written him asking for authentic biographical information, "they are, I suppose, easily accessible to anyone. Beyond that, I do not know that any account of my life or thoughts has ever been written. I have avoided with some persistence both biography and autobiography. None except of my own household has ever come near enough to me for the former and I have small inclination for the latter."

The above statement must be taken with the classic grain of salt, however; for though it is in the main correct, its author did begin an account of his life which, as he noted on the margin of the manuscript, was intended for use as the basis of a biography to be written by one of his closest friends. He also left several other autobiographical accounts of certain periods of his life, and from them many of the facts in this biography have been taken.

The Tourgée family, of Huguenot origin, left France in 1685, following the Revocation of the Edict of Nantes. After stopping for a brief period on the Island of Guernsey, its members decided to break the last chain that held them to the Old World, and accordingly settled in Kingston, Rhode Island, in the latter part of the seventeenth century. The first Tourgée whose name is left on record was Peter, who supported himself and family in this part of the New World by peg and awl. At some indefinite period in the early eighteenth century the family again moved, this time to Framingham, Massachusetts, and there the future author's grandfather, Valentine Tourgée, married Rebecka Robbins, whose family had come from New London, Connecticut, after experiencing the siege of that town by the traitor Benedict Arnold. To this couple was born Valentine Jr., father of Albion W. Tourgée, in 1814. During his early manhood Valentine the second moved to Lee, Berkshire County, Massachusetts, and there met Louisa Emma Winegar, who was a descendant of Edward Doty, one of the famous colony that came over on the *Mayflower*. The Winegar family was of German origin, and the first one whose name is known, Ulric Winegar, born in Switzerland in 1648, came to America in 1710 with the colony of Palatines which was under the fostering care of Queen Anne. Ulric settled in Ulster County, New York, and at some later date moved to Lee, where, as has been noted, Valentine Tourgée Jr. had likewise come. Jacob Winegar, maternal grandfather of Albion W. Tourgée, had a family of seven children; one,

Jack, was a member of the Massachusetts Legislature, and another, Jacob Jr., was apparently a happy-go-lucky chap, which may account for the fact that his youthful nephew, Albion, came to him in the forties, for the comforts of home which his carping stepmother denied him.

It was at Lee, Massachusetts, then, that the author's parents met. His father was here engaged in the manufacture of paper. In 1836 he married Louisa Emma Winegar, his brother Cyrus and one of Louisa's four sisters also marrying at the same time. Apparently the nomadic instincts which had characterized both families were inherited by these descendants, for both couples soon after the joint marriage removed to Williamsfield, Ashtabula County, Ohio, where Valentine and Louisa Tourgée settled on a farm. And here, on May 2, 1838, was born their first child, Albion Winegar Tourgée. Two other children were born to them, but both died in infancy. The author's mother, never strong, gradually wasted away and finally died of tuberculosis in February, 1843. All that he was ever able to recall of his mother was that she used to whip him gently because he "toed in," and that her funeral took place on a bleak winter's day.

The bereaved husband and father bore this calamity bravely and for several years remained alone with his baby son. He finally decided to tempt fate, however, by procuring a foster mother for his child, and accordingly took a second spouse, Rowena Snow, some time between 1844 and 1846, to which union there was born a daughter about ten years Albion's junior. In 1847 a final removal was made to a farm one and a half miles north of Kingsville, Ohio, and here the father, who had seen his son grow famous, died April 26, 1889. Meanwhile fate, having been tempted, was proving capricious as usual, for the boy's legal mother was showing herself true to the well-fixed tradition of her species.[1] The result was that the high-spirited lad, who, by the time he was fourteen, was already beginning to show that uncompromising independence which later became one of the most pronounced characteristics of the grown man, decided to sever connections with his home and go for protection and solace to his uncle, Jacob Winegar Jr., in Lee, Massachusetts. How he obtained the funds for this youthful adventure is not known, but obtain them he did and stayed in his new home apparently for some two years. The facts about this period of his life are very meagre indeed, but probably he was pleased with the Rip Van Winkle propensities of his uncle; for in one of his autobiographical fragments Tourgée boasts that as a boy he could never be relied on to perform the farm chores which his father assigned him, but that he usually stole the paternal rifle and hied him to the woods to return just when he pleased. It is only fair to state, however, that the chief element of interest in the prodigal's

[1] This characterization of Tourgée's step-mother is based wholly upon his own statement about her. A lady who knew Rowena Snow Tourgée intimately has assured me, however, that she was in reality a "mild, even-tempered woman, who always spoke very quietly." Tourgée probably magnified whatever faults his step-mother may have had, in accordance with his usual practice of exaggerating the hardships of his career.

return was an irate parent "armed with retributory cudgel." The use of the rod was of course firmly believed in, because the lad's father was a very strict Methodist, whose enormously long supplications in the weekly prayer meetings could, according to tradition, be heard far beyond the walls of the church itself. The Methodistic element in the father's character also showed itself in his love of argument, which was in turn inherited by his son. Often the two would, in the midst of a tempestuous debate, seat themselves at the table, when, of course, it was necessary to pause briefly for the saying of grace; and once this perfunctory task had been performed as speedily as possible, the verbal combat would be renewed with greater violence than ever.

But, though he loved rod and gun with all the fervor of youth, the boy loved books as well, and it was at the library in Lee that his first real opportunity for extensive reading came. His father had once intended to prepare for a profession and had bought many books with this end in view. But financial loss, and more particularly a strong religious awakening, had turned his mind from such worldly pursuits as the mastering of professions, and also the making of verse, in which he had occasionally indulged; hence it was that religious zeal prompted him to commit to the flames such impious performances as Scott's novels and other works of a like nature. The following volumes had been preserved, however, for their indubitable moral qualities, and had been read by Albion in lieu of more exciting material: the Bible, Goodrich's "Universal

History," a "History of the United States," "Pilgrim's Progress," Bacon's "Essays," "Paradise Lost," "Night Thoughts," D'Aubigne's "History of the Reformation," other historical works, a book of fables, the ubiquitous "Scottish Chiefs," and some volumes of religious biography. The boy was compelled to memorize parts of "Paradise Lost," "Night Thoughts," and the Bible for his soul's good and incidentally as a punishment for childish offences. He liked the Gospel of St. John, the Acts of the Apostles, and the Revelations especially well, and once said that he could have restored all three of these had all copies been lost; but it may justly be surmised that he was here emulating a commonly known statement of Macaulay, rather than telling the facts of the case. This, then, had constituted his intellectual pabulum till the good New England library opened his eyes to a much more extensive literary field; and from this time till the call to arms came, he literally reveled in English literature, while it is significant that he was particularly interested in history and the background of fiction—the life and society of the times portrayed.

At some indefinite period, probably in 1854, he returned to his father's farm; for, being now nearly full-grown, he had little cause to fear the weight of his father's arm and still less his step-mother's tongue. He was somewhat undersized for his age at this time, but very tough and wiry. Here he remained, alternately teaching in some elementary school and studying at Kingsville Academy, whither he daily trudged from the home farm until he entered the University of

Rochester in 1859. This academy had as its principal
Chester W. Heywood, a young man fresh from college, to whom Tourgée became warmly attached and
to whom he always gave precedence later when speaking of the formative influences of his early life. Heywood freely opened his quite extensive library to the
boy, and thus further literary treasures were revealed
to him. Particularly, at this time, he read the Waver-
ley novels, taking one home every other day till he had
finished the set. Meanwhile, "Al," as he was familiarly
called, was rapidly winning first place as a scholar, despite the fact that the standard of attainment at the
academy was high, since attendance was voluntary and
most of the students were paying their own way. He
was regarded by his fellow students as destined for a
brilliant career because of his general scholastic ability,
especially in languages. It was at this time that he
formed the determination to follow the legal profession.

During his academy days, the future novelist had
already begun to exercise his 'prentice pen in a very
'prentice manner indeed. A manuscript book of his,
dated March, 1857, and entitled "Sense and Non-
sense," contains these first endeavors, and it is perhaps no more than charitable to remark that the non-
sense is far more in evidence that any glimmerings of
sense. There are about forty "poems," some based
upon classical subjects and written in a very weak
Byronic style; in fact, two are addressed to that
poet so often imitated by aspiring youths. Apparently
some of these verses sought immortality by being

printed in the academy paper. But by far the larger
part of these rhymed lines bear the title To Emma,
and since she will appear very frequently in the pages
that follow, it may be well to know something about
her now.

The young lady thus poetically eulogized was Emma
Lodoiska Kilbourne, the daughter of Harmon and
Mary Corwin Kilbourne, and she was likewise a student at Kingsville Academy. Both the Kilbourne and
Corwin families were descended from Yorkshire gen-
try, and had come to New England before 1635. Some
of their descendants had intermarried with the Win-
throps of Massachusetts, and as a result Emma Kilbourne was a lineal descendant of both governors of
that name. The Kilbournes settled in Bristol, Ver-
mont; and after the Revolutionary War, since they
were suspected of being too fond of the Tories to be
comfortable in New England, they emigrated to Canada, whence at some later time they removed to Con-
neaut, Ohio. At this place it was that Emma lived,
and whence she was sent to the academy. It was a
case of love at first sight, on Tourgée's part at least;
for when he first saw her, he confidentially remarked to
a friend, "I'm going to marry that girl," and after an
engagement of five years he did so. The remark he
made to her on his death bed, "Emma, you have been
the one perfect wife," was but little exaggerated, as
succeeding events will show.

After ending his academy days, Tourgée probably
taught school a little while, and then, from the autumn
of 1859 till January, 1861, he was a student at the Uni-

versity of Rochester. Just before entering this institution, he made another trip to Lee, Massachusetts, to receive his share of his grandfather's property; the amount of his share is unknown, but it certainly was not large, for he paid his own way through college. Had he chosen to do so, he might have had his college expenses paid by another; for during his boyhood stay in Lee, a gentleman there had been so impressed by Tourgée's youthful promise that he later offered to send him to Williams College. But, independent as usual, Tourgée refused this kind offer and went to Rochester, where he received sophomore rating, doubtless because of his good record at the academy.

Here he made no special effort to attain high scholastic standing, but largely followed his own sweet will. His course was very erratic; what he read, he read with all his might, but in the subjects that interested him least, he did just enough work to maintain his standing in class. He read poetry enormously, but mathematics was his special aversion. One day his mathematics teacher reprimanded him for a poor recitation, whereupon with tears in his eyes he blurted out: "Professor! I like you personally better than any man on the faculty, but I don't like mathematics and I won't study them if I have to leave college." He read all of Shakspere and, if we can believe his word, all the pre-Shaksperean dramatists, to see how great their influence on the master dramatist had been. He had a habit of marking the books in the college library with his own pen, but this peccadillo was not discovered until he had become so famous that the books thus marked gained added value in the eyes of the college authorities by reason of these disfigurements. He was fond of debating in his college days, and has left in manuscript some specimens of his speeches, which are couched in the usual terms of forensic finality that one ordinarily finds in the philippics of a budding orator. A manuscript book containing notes on a college course in logic has also about a dozen more poems, several of them having war as their theme, which uniformly maintain the high standard of inferiority that had characterized those written in his academy days. This same manuscript book contains also some fragments of short stories. More significant than any of these interests were his friendships with the students, and particularly with President M. B. Anderson, who was Tourgée's life-long friend and counselor.

As soon as the first mutterings of the fast approaching war were heard, Tourgée began to show that love of leadership which was always one of his strong traits by organizing a number of students and drilling them. He amply proved his mastery one day, when one of the members of his "company," a close friend of his, did something which displeased him. In a very short space of time, the friend was on the ground with the self-appointed officer on top, pummelling him unmercifully. Apparently his funds were running low at this time, for in January, 1861, he left the University and became associate principal of a school at Wilson, Niagara County, New York. He doubtless intended to return to his collegiate work at some future time, but it was not to be. The degree of A.B. was granted to him by the University in June, 1862, however, in accordance with the common practice of awarding degrees to students who had entered the service of their country before their academic careers were quite completed. Years later, in 1880 to be exact, Rochester University awarded him the honorary degree of LL.D., and three years later the University of Copenhagen made him a Doctor of Philosophy. Tourgée remained at the school in Wilson until the nineteenth of April, 1861, on which date he enlisted in the 27th New York Volunteers.

He had not long to wait before suffering for the cause of the Union. In the first Battle of Bull Run, on July 4, 1861, he lost the sight of his left eye [1] and also received a bad wound in his spine. The eye was later removed and a glass one put in its place, which so closely resembled the natural one that many people who knew him fairly well never suspected that his left eye was artificial. But the wound to the spine was a different matter. During the whole of his life he never fully recovered from it, for it caused a permanent nervousness and often excruciating pain; consequently, he never saw a really well day after that eventful fourth of July.

[1] Tourgée stated again and again in his writings that his left eye was lost in this battle; but some of his intimate friends, whose word is unimpeachable, have assured me that in reality he had already lost the sight of this eye by an accident in his boyhood. It seems plain that in this case, as in several others, Tourgée was so enthralled by his ultra-romantic theory of life, which colored all he did and wrote, that he applied it to one of the rather drab facts of his actual career.

For three days after this tragic event Tourgée was in a state of coma, and when he returned to consciousness it was to find himself in Washington with a nurse at his side. The roar of battle was still in his ears, and for several weeks he lived over, in his dilirium, the ghastly events of that momentous day. The surgeon in attendance looked for nothing for him save a slow lingering until death should mercifully come. But instead he began gradually to mend, though it was eleven months before he could walk without the aid of crutches. By August, 1861, he had recovered sufficient vitality to become somewhat entranced by a Washington belle, a guest at the house where he was invalided; but as soon as he saw Miss Kilbourne once more, to whom he had been engaged for three years, his old love returned stronger than ever. In this month, having received his honorable discharge from the army, he was sent to Ashtabula, Ohio, lying on the floor of the train that carried him, for his back was too weak to permit his sitting up. Having arrived at Ashtabula, he lay on his couch and read Blackstone every day, until, by January, 1862, he was able to hobble on crutches down to the law office of Sherman & Farmer, Ashtabula, where he studied law till the following July.

But what of his literary work during this period? The answer is that it saw the publication of his first book, and the circumstances of this event are of sufficient interest to warrant narration. Before this story is told, however, it should be noted that, when Tourgée started for war, he had in his knapsack two volumes, a Greek Testament and Cicero's "De Natura Deorum."

The Testament was included not because of any particular religious motive, but simply because he wished to continue the study of Greek. But he took the other book because he really liked to read it (he always excelled in Latin), having already read it more than once. During his army life he read both these books several times, and the Testament was especially welcome to his closest friend in the army, a theological student. Tourgée also read during his first army experience parts of the "Comédie Humaine" in the original.

At the time when he began as a cripple to study law, Tourgée had already written a few stories which had appeared in some cheap periodicals long since gone into the limbo of oblivion, and he had even received a little pay for some of them; but so far he had no thought of literature as a serious occupation. Now, however, with the prospect of being a permanent invalid, possibly always confined to a couch, the thought of writing came to him, and he was materially assisted in this direction by the advice of President Anderson of Rochester and of the Professor of Greek in that institution. Acting upon their advice, he made the synopsis and indeed wrote several chapters of a novel; but he finally decided instead to publish a volume of poems, most of which had already been written. One more, however, he was prompted to write, and it is worthy of remark that it was concerned with the conditions attending the outbreak of the Civil War. At this lengthy poem he labored until its completion in January, 1862. Then, as soon as he was able, he journeyed to a neighboring city to seek a publisher. He found one who was willing to execute his wishes, provided that he would assume the cost of the job. Tourgée assented, thinking that he could pay for it with the money from the pension that had just been granted him, a pension which he renounced upon patriotic motives when he re-entered the service. But the book, published under an assumed name, cost all the pension money and a little more. When he received the first two copies sent him by the publisher, he was so disappointed at the immaturity which, hidden in the hypnotizing manuscript, the printed pages revealed, that he thrust them with small delay into the kitchen stove. This incineration was also determined upon partly because of the advice of his father, to whom he had shown the volumes in hope of winning some paternal praise. Late in the summer of 1862, he went to the publisher for a report and found that of the one hundred copies printed twenty had been sold. He had not at any time really expected that the sale of the book would entirely pay for the expenses of publication; but by this time no illusion whatever, either literary or financial, remained; and accordingly he sought and obtained permission from the publisher to cut the unsold copies into bits, which he did, not, however, without some pangs of regret. Nevertheless, he had now tasted both the sweets and pains of authorship; and, while it was easy to destroy this first product of his enthusiasm for literature, the enthusiasm itself remained, dormant for some years, to be sure, by reason of war, bad health, and the necessity of earning a living, but still it remained.

Meanwhile sterner events were again claiming Tourgée's active interest. During the spring of 1862, he took a preparation containing strychnia and thereupon began to recover the use of his limbs. While still an invalid, he attended meetings for the recruiting of volunteers and even spoke for their cause, seated in a chair. By July he was again well enough to serve his country, and accordingly went to Columbus and got a commission as first lieutenant in Company G of the 105th Ohio Volunteers, many of whose members were his old academy schoolmates. Over thirty years later, in "The Story of a Thousand," he performed a labor of love by giving a minute account of this company. Unfortunately for his biographer, he, as the preface states, "endeavored to restrict personal incident almost entirely to illustrative events common to the experience of all"; hence it was that he did not describe his own experiences in prison because they were too personal "to be compatible with the general tone of the work." From July till October the company was engaged in minor war activities in Kentucky. At the Battle of Perryville, October 8, 1862, however, it lost about one-third of its total strength, and Tourgée again suffered an injury to his spine which kept him in a hospital at Danville, Kentucky, through October and November. He rejoined his company about the first of December and for the next month spent his time in helping to chase the raider Morgan.

It was during this time that an event of special

interest occurred, best told in Tourgée's own words. "I remember that as late as September 1862, I was myself put under arrest in the army of the United States, for refusing to surrender a colored man who had saved my company."[1] This brief utterance, concerning a fact of which nothing else is known, is the first evidence of that consuming passion which later influenced nearly everything Tourgée did and wrote— an untiring sympathy, admiration, even love, for the negro in his servile·state, and a zeal which was never quenched for obtaining justice (at least Tourgée's conception of justice) for the black man.

At some time in January, 1863, another event took place of which little but the bare statement of fact is known. On one of the Morgan expeditions referred to, Tourgée was captured at Murfreesboro, Tennessee, and spent the following four months in prison. He has left little record of this decidedly unpleasant episode in his life, but it is certain that, in what order is unknown, the several walls of the prisons at Atlanta, Milan, Salisbury, and those of the notorious Libby, encased him. He later referred to this experience as follows: "Despite the temptation, he [Tourgée] has rarely alluded to the fact that he was a guest of 'Libby' and sundry other hotels of that type—only more so— at the South, in public speech or writing. . . . Of the treatment they received, the lack of supplies, the crowded condition of the prisons, the lack of shelter, the inexpressible foulness of some of them, and the

[1] *The Chautauquan,* Nov. 1881, p. 93.

indifference manifested toward their feelings, he has said nothing lest his purpose should be misconceived." [1] Decidedly uncomfortable as these experiences were, their irksome monotony must have been slightly mitigated by at least three changes of air and "scenery." In later years he once remarked to a friend, apropos of this experience: "I ran away once or twice and was shot at, caught and penned up again. Oh, I had quite a variety." He put some part of his life in prison to good account by the study of Spanish and the attendant reading of Cervantes's immortal tale in the original, together with Carlyle's "French Revolution," which was "one of the few books that found their way into the room in Libby Prison of which the Bystander was at one time joint-tenant with many others." [2] But in the first part of May, 1863, he was exchanged from prison, and so freed from one of the most disagreeable misfortunes that can happen to a soldier.

That he wasted little time in returning home and becoming partner in an event which he and another person had longingly anticipated for five years, is sufficiently evinced by the following passage taken from his war diary, which covers the period from May till November, 1863, and which has fortunately been preserved: "May 14, 1863. Married at Columbus, Ohio, by the Rev. Julius E. Gardner at the Med. Coll. buildings. Returned to our lodgings in the W. S. Hotel

[1] "A Bystander's Notes," in *The Chicago Inter Ocean*, Feb. 13, 1890.
[2] *Ibid.*, June 26, 1891.

to take life quietly and happily. It ought to be happy, for it is the consummation of five years of pleasant waiting and sweet expectation." But unfortunately the quiet and happy life was not destined to last long at that particular time, for the diary on May 25 contains this terse sentence: "To-day I left for the war again."

Practically the only source of information about Tourgée's life during the remainder of this year is this same war diary, together with some passages in "The Story of a Thousand." There is little of worth in this much battered diary except as it contains biographical information, for its contents are merely typical of most personal records of this kind. It is filled with grumblings at army life and its privations on the one hand, and fervidly patriotic sentiments on the other, complaints of the scarcity of letters, and particularly many devout expressions of love for his wife and supplications to the Almighty that he may be spared to return to her in safety. Much of it was written in the blackness of night as its sprawling, at times illegible, lines show, not a little during pauses between battles, and some even while he was directly under fire. The following passage is characteristic: "July 5. We got a mail today but nothing for me. Well no wonder for Emma has gone on a spree and cannot stop to write to me. I do hope the darling is happy."

"The Story of a Thousand" gives a much clearer idea of the army activities in which Tourgée took part during this time than does the diary. From this history it is apparent that the 105th Ohio Volunteers was engaged in several battles. During the latter part of June, this regiment was among those which saw action in the campaign against the Confederate position at Tullahoma, which was taken July 1. It also assisted in the Battle of Chickamauga and in the campaign against Chattanooga. Moreover, it saw service in the victorious battles of Lookout Mountain and Missionary Ridge. Its subsequent participation in the march "from Atlanta to the sea" was not, however, shared by Tourgée, as will shortly appear.

It has been noted that Tourgée had already been under arrest in 1862, and his second experience of the kind came in June, 1863. The diary states that during this month he was in prison two weeks because, while on picket duty, he had pricked with his sword a soldier who had tried to get through the lines, and was accordingly accused of wounding him. After being incarcerated two weeks, Tourgée was released from prison, but the charge against him was not finally disposed of until several weeks later. He was sentenced to be formally reprimanded by his superior officer; but that the reprimand was only a form is evident from the language in which, according to the diary, it was couched: "Lieutenant Tourgée, I have nothing to say. You will report for duty tomorrow morning."

To take commands from another was the one thing that galled Tourgée perhaps more than anything else. On June 2 he tendered his resignation as first lieutenant because his "rights were not respected and his reputation threatened," but it was not accepted. It was doubtless this independence of spirit, combined with his interest in the negro which had already manifested itself, that led him during the following summer to meditate withdrawal from his regiment and the formation of a negro company, to be officered of course by himself. And it was probably because of this same independence, together with the fact that his old wound (which had already troubled him much of the time) was aggravated when he leapt a ditch in October, that he applied for leave of absence. This he apparently obtained about the tenth of November, for his diary closes on that date, while he was waiting for his leave of absence and feeling very wretched on account of his wound. In December he again tendered his resignation because of insolence (at least he called it such) on the part of his superiors, which was once more not accepted. Whether it was finally accepted because of this friction or because of his state of health is not definitely known; at any rate, on about January 1, 1864, he withdrew from the army. The fact probably is that what Tourgée deemed to be independence was regarded as pig-headedness by his superior officers, and probability strongly favors their opinion.

Upon thus severing his connection with the army, Tourgée without doubt at once went home, though the next five months are a blank as far as definite facts are concerned. At all events, on May 2, 1864, the anniversary of his birth in a month which he always regarded as peculiarly lucky for him, he was admitted to the bar at Painsville, Ohio, and at once entered the law office of the firm with which he had previously studied, Sherman & Farmer. On July 2, licenses to practise law and to act as Claim Agent were granted him at Ashtabula, Ohio. Here there is another gap in biographic facts and a jump of eight months must be made, during which time he was doubtless increasing his knowledge of law, acquiring some financial rewards, and enjoying marital felicity. The jump just referred to ends in March, 1865, when for some reason he became a teacher in Erie Academy, Erie, Pennsylvania, where he remained till the end of the school year. He also did some writing for *The Erie Dispatch* during this time. It is also possible that, at some time during the spring or early summer of this year, he sought and obtained the rank of major of a colored regiment, and that he was on his way to resume his war activities when the end of the struggle made any future military career for him impossible. Certainly there is every reason to believe that such a command would have been very acceptable to him, had his health been good enough to make such an honor possible, although this is very doubtful.

For the time was now nearly at hand when, principally on account of his health, Tourgée was to take the step which proved to be far more important in its consequences than all the events of his life thus far put together. In fact, had he not embarked on this enterprise, it is very doubtful if any but his immediate friends would ever have remembered his name, or any account of his life been thought of sufficient value and interest to be recorded.

CHAPTER II

THE SOUTH

In July, 1865, Tourgée went South alone to seek a new home for himself and his wife. His precarious health was, as already stated, the chief motive for this venture, for his spinal wound, the general hardship of life in the army, together with a weakness of the lungs which was probably inherited from his mother, had all combined to make him anything but robust at this time. For several weeks he was engaged as counsel in a court martial then being held at Raleigh, North Carolina, and for the next few weeks he made an extensive tour through that state and Georgia also to seek a permanent residence near the Atlantic seacoast. Greensboro, North Carolina, was the locality finally selected, partly because he liked the place as well as any he had seen, and also because he was there able to rent the West Green Nurseries from C. P. Mendenhall—for he had decided to engage in the nursery business as well as in his regular profession. Having thus brought to a successful conclusion his search for a home better adapted to his state of health, he returned to Ohio in the latter part of August. The next few weeks were spent in settling his business affairs, and the fourteenth of October found him and his wife in Greensboro with a capital of $5000 acquired through his legal activities.

And so, from being a respected citizen of the North, in whose recent victoriously concluded cause he was an honored veteran, Tourgée became not a citizen but a "carpet-bagger" in the denuded, poverty-stricken South, whose wounds were still unstanched, whose efficient white male population was almost wiped out, whose territory was teeming with recently liberated, hence inexpressibly despised, negroes, and whose proud spirit, smarting with the sense of intolerable defeat, regarded almost everything Northern with fearful hatred.

It is not the purpose of this biography to discuss in detail the Reconstruction Period, for that has already been done for the South as a whole[1] and for the part in which Tourgée lived in particular.[2] The interest in this discussion lies in the special part played by him in this movement, and the indelible results of this experience which showed themselves in his character and in his writings.

Picture the situation. To this land, a land cursed by war, pestilence and famine, came this youthful,

[1] "History of the United States," by James Ford Rhodes, The Macmillan Co., New York, 1906, Vols. 6 and 7. Also "The American Nation: A History;" General Editor A. B. Hart; Vol. 23, "Reconstruction Political and Social, 1865-1877," by W. A. Dunning, Harper & Brothers, 1907.

[2] Columbia University Dissertation, "Reconstruction in North Carolina," by J. G. de Roulhac Hamilton, Edwards & Broughton, Raleigh, N. C., 1906.

impetuous, headstrong lawyer who believed in himself
and the cause of the North absolutely without reserve,
and who did not, at least in his early years, know the
meaning of the words prudence and restraint. This
being true, there could be but one result: enemies on
every hand, both of reputation and life itself, oppro-
brium, and what amounted practically to social
ostracism, save for the friendship of the negroes, the
handful of carpet-baggers, and a comparatively few
Southerners, mostly Republicans, whose sympathies
were not wholly with their native land. This, then, is
in general what Tourgée experienced during the next
fourteen years; a detailed account of the specific occurrences in his life during this period follows.

As has been noted, Tourgée began his life here by
engaging in the nursery business. After a few months
of conducting the enterprise alone, during which time
he also practised law, he decided that an increase of
capital as well as other tangible assistance was advisable. There is still extant a contract dated March
16, 1866, which reveals that at that time a firm was
organized by Tourgée, Seneca Kuhn of Greensboro,
and R. L. Pettingill, formerly of Rochester, with a
joint capital of $4500 in three equal shares, to be
known as the Tourgée, Kuhn & Pettingill Firm, for
the purpose of conducting the nursery business. Probably this same triumvirate also practised law together
under the name of A. W. Tourgée & Co., although it
is not certain that Pettingill was a partner. But the
bonds apparently thus firmly forged were soon broken,
for Pettingill withdrew from the nursery firm in the

following summer, and Kuhn followed suit on December 6, 1866. Soon after this, Tourgée and Kuhn also dissolved the ties of legal partnership. The exact reasons for these dissolutions are not definitely known, though Tourgée later referred to Kuhn as a "rascal," apparently because he appropriated certain funds to himself; but this being a favorite derogatory epithet of Tourgée's, it is perhaps best to state the mere facts and not attempt to draw conclusions. At all events, there is a sudden cessation at this time of any further information about the nursery business, whereas there is abundance of evidence that ere long Tourgée was hard pressed for money; and by June, 1867, the nursery venture had found an early grave, while Tourgée was left several thousand dollars in debt.

During the year 1866 he had already begun that fearless and imprudent course of unceasing criticism of all things Southern that marked his whole subsequent career. He was a delegate to the Loyalist Convention held at Philadelphia in September, which "was designed to bring about a demonstration by the thick-and-thin opponents of secession and Confederacy, who, through the operation of Johnson's policy, had been overwhelmed in their respective states by the popular ex-Confederates." [1] At this convention he delivered a speech in which he bitterly assailed the South for its treatment of the negro. This, together with other utterances of a similar unqualified nature, led to his receiving the first of a series of anonymous

[1] "Reconstruction Political and Social," by W. A. Dunning, p. 77.

letters, which from that time on were showered upon him during his stay in the South. Several of these made the customary threat of giving him a coat of tar and feathers if his "lying tung," as one epistle put it, was not stopped. Some of them were, however, friendly letters warning him for the sake of personal safety to be discreet or else leave the South. But threats or words of friendly counsel equally failed to move him, though in the following year he took the wise precaution of requesting and obtaining permission to carry firearms for personal protection.

Meanwhile, undaunted by disrupted partnerships and the imminent failure of his nursery, the irrepressible Tourgée, whose faith in all sorts of financial will-o-the-wisps seemed to grow stronger every time it was knocked topsy-turvy, was already forming a new enterprise even before the final failure of his first business experience. He had probably been engaged in the real estate business in 1866, possibly again with a partner; at any rate, the statement that the first half of the year 1867 saw him embarked on his first journalistic venture fortunately needs no qualification. On January 3, 1867, there appeared the first edition of *The Union Register,* published by the Union Publishing Company at Greensboro. This was a weekly newspaper containing four very large pages of seven columns each, which sold for three dollars per year. While Tourgée's name does not appear directly in print as editor of this paper, its editor he unquestionably was; and the following utterance, taken from the editorial of the first number and explaining the function of the paper, is with little doubt his own pronouncement: "We are aware that the advocacy of Union principles; or, if you prefer the word, radical principles, is anything but a popular movement in any part of the South. It is what we have enlisted for, however. . . . Let us . . . give our strength to loose it [the South] from the slough of ignorance and prejudice." This same editorial also speaks of the "poor, misguided and mismanaged South." An editorial on January 25 also gives the unnecessary information that "the *Register* hopes never to be a 'mild' advocate of anything"; for if Tourgée ever reiterated his entire lack of lukewarmness once, he did it a thousand times. It would seem that the statement of the first editorial to the effect that the advocacy of Union principles was anything but a popular Southern movement had amply proved itself by the following June, for an editorial on the fourteenth of that month states that the "present number of the *Register* is the last which will be published in its present locality. . . . Six months ago, under every possible form of discouragement, the *Register* sprang into life, the unfaltering champion of true and absolute Republicanism. . . . The hundreds of North Carolinians who are patrons of the *Register* may be regarded as the forlorn hope of true Republicanism in the state." Other editorials had advocated the principles which Tourgée fought for in the convention the following year. The paper was transferred to Raleigh under different management, to which place it is probable that the "forlorn hope" sent many letters of inquiry as to the fate of the three dollars which had been invested by many Republicans in a year's subscription. Thus ended in failure another of Tourgée's attempts to succeed in an undertaking which required the "head for business" he did not have. That it was a failure, though partly because of extraneous reasons, is sufficiently attested in his own words, in a letter dated April 2, 1868: "I started one newspaper here at Greensboro—the *Register*—and it ran on until, by exterior mishaps, I lost all I had brought here." This is probably a reference to the nursery fiasco; at any rate, the newspaper was not successful, and it is doubtful if it paid for the cost of its production. These various enterprises of his, however, failures though they had been, combined to make him a fairly prominent figure in the public eye.

Tourgée was already forming the habit of making speeches whenever opportunity offered, in which he was apparently utterly reckless of the effects of his statements on the feelings of his audience. A Southern gentleman later commented thus on one of these speeches delivered at Greensboro: "He let fly a speech at Andrew Johnson which, I reckon, made him the most hated man in all that community. He said he was worse than Catiline; that he was no improvement on Jefferson Davis, etc. While we all listened in speechless disgust, I couldn't help admiring the persistence and pluck of the little devil." [1]

Hated or not, however, the "little devil" would have been appointed Judge of the Superior Court, Seventh

[1] *New York Tribune,* April 4, 1881.

Judicial District of North Carolina, in the early part of 1867, had it not been for the bitterness entertained against him by the governor of the state, Jonathan Worth, who had read Tourgée's speech which had been delivered at the Loyalist Convention in Philadelphia in September, 1866, and who now attacked him vehemently for its statements about Southern atrocities against the negro. Governor Worth in his correspondence gives vent to his opinions about Tourgée in the following language: "Tourgée, the meanest Yankee who has ever settled among us";[1] "this vile wretch Tourgée";[2] "this contemptible Tourgée"[3] and, perhaps most scathing of all, simply, "this Tourgée."[4]   In giving his reasons for objecting to Tourgée as a judge, Worth says: "I am sure I have heard more than 100 men speak of Tourgée as a man of 'most contemptible character' and I never heard one speak well of him."[5]   The irascible governor also stated on May 26, 1868, that Tourgée had "never practised law in this state nor had a license to practise";[6] but this statement was incorrect, for in a letter to the Paymaster General at Washington, March 23, 1868, Tourgée says that he has held a license to practise since 1867, and objects against being taxed for a new license.   But the doughty governor's opposition

[1] "The Correspondence of Jonathan Worth," collected and edited by J. G. de Roulhac Hamilton, Raleigh, Edwards & Broughton, 1909. Two vols. Vol. II, p. 1120.
[2] *Ibid.*, p. 776.
[3] *Ibid.*, 777.
[4] *Ibid.*
[5] *Ibid.*, 1114.
[6] *Ibid.*, 1213.

to Tourgée as a judge had merely the effect of post-
poning that event only a little over a year; for on
March 21, 1868, Tourgée wrote a letter accepting the
nomination for the office of judge, and in the election
which followed he was put in the office by a majority
of over twenty-five thousand.

Before this personal triumph, however, an event took
place with which Tourgée's name is closely associated.
On January 14, 1868, a Constitutional Convention met
at Raleigh and one of the members was Tourgée. The
delegation included 13 Conservatives, 107 Republicans
(of whom 16 were carpet-baggers) and 13 negroes.[1]
Hence it was that "Individually and collectively the
'carpet-baggers' controlled the convention absolutely."[2]
Tourgée himself advocated that the entire state debt
of the new North Carolina should be repudiated. But
this doctrine was too strong for the majority, being attacked even by three colored delegates, and so was
defeated.[3] He was, however, appointed one of three
commissioners for a term of three years at a salary
of $200 a month to codify the laws of the State.[4] In
this capacity he was the chief figure in putting into
organic law the Code of Civil Procedure, largely a
Northern idea, copied from the codes of New York
and Ohio. This code was of course strongly opposed
by some Southern lawyers, but finally proved its worth,

[1] "Reconstruction in North Carolina," Hamilton, p. 229.
[2] *Ibid.*, 237.
[3] *Ibid.*, 238.
[4] *Ibid.*, 239.

since it was much less cumbersome than the old code had been.

The following excerpts from a letter of Tourgée's to his daughter, dated February 1, 1890, will serve to show his own reaction to this convention, to his election as judge, and to his first literary work of importance: "The fear of starvation and shame led me to fight for a place as a member of the Constitutional Convention of 1868. I found myself the strongest man in it. I suffered almost mortal agony over the task of undertaking the duties of the Judgeship in 1868. It was easy to me and I won honor in it. . . . I do not suppose any one who knew me would have advised me to get an election to the Convention, to accept the Judgeship, or to write 'Toinette.' They are the three things on which my successes are all based."

Whatever may be thought of the tone of this letter, written to show his daughter the necessity of following one's own star and of making decisions without waiting for advice, it is certain that many Southern gentlemen would not have advised him to do any of the above things. One of them would doubtless have been the person referred to in a letter of Tourgée's dated April 2, 1868: "You would have been in danger of spasms if you had seen me drop a platter over an opponent's pate at a public dinner last week. He called me a 'rascal.' Of course I cared not a flea-bite for his words, but if I had not resented them the crowd would have set me down as a coward. So I was fool enough to do it." This first "fool's errand" episode of which there is any mention doubtless refers to his campaign as a candidate for the office of judge, and the incident related is but one of many in a campaign of general vilification on both sides. It seems that Governor Worth was still on the war-path, for in a private letter dated April 15, 1868, Tourgée says: "I happen, to know that Governor Worth used every inducement to get some of my enemies here to slander me. . . . I intend to make the old scoundrel smart for it some time and perhaps some others." One type of slander directed at him was the deliberate charge, printed by several newspapers, that he had been in an Ohio prison four and one half years for burglary. This malicious lie Tourgée at once indignantly denied and offered a reward of $1000 to anyone who could show tangible evidence connecting him with such guilt. It is more than doubtful if he could have paid such a sum at that particular time, but he was of course aware that he was safe in offering to do so. His usual method of answering these assaults upon his character, whether in his private letters or in articles intended for publication, was to state that such low, mean, contemptible reptiles as those who were attacking him deserved only silent contempt; and he would then forthwith proceed to dig up every scurrilous adjective he could think of to hurl at their heads, silently contemptuous for anywhere from five to thirty pages.

In spite of these numerous enemies of his, however, Tourgée was elected judge and began his duties in August, 1868, duties which occupied his time for the next six years. As his jurisdiction extended over eight counties, he was absent from home much of the time. The $5000 per year which his office paid him, together with the money received for helping codify the laws of the state, enabled him in the following year to pay off the still remaining debts of Tourgée & Co., as well as to purchase a house and lot on Asheboro Street for $3500, which was probably a welcome change for him and his wife after their life on the nursery farm about four miles west of Greensboro. But that he still considered himself underpaid for his services on the bench is sufficiently attested by a document drawn up by him in July, 1868, entitled "Reasons for the Increase of Judges' Salaries," a document which would probably never have seen the light of day had he not himself been a judge.

It was during the period in which he was judge that Tourgée experienced the most exciting events of his more than ordinarily exciting career. There can be little question that his life was in almost constant danger during this time. The chief factor in this was of course the notorious Ku Klux Klan, the secret organization which history and tradition have made so familiar as to need no discussion here. Tourgée, with his uncompromising carpet-bagger traits, which were shown in giving preference to negroes over whites whenever suitable opportunity offered, was a perfectly natural object for its attack. His private letters during this period abound in references to the active hostility which this terrorizing band manifested against him. He received many notices which definitely fixed the time when he was to be assassinated, as well as a paper,

pinned by a knife to his door, on which was a picture
of a coffin and a written notice that he was doomed to
an agonizing death. On one occasion the place fixed
for his assassination was the room in which he was
holding court, the murder to be done after he had
finished speaking and had turned his back to retire
through a door in the rear. Luckily the plot was revealed to him and he held court all the morning, to all
appearances as unconcernedly as ever; but when he had
completed the morning's work, instead of retiring to
the rear, he walked straight through the crowded
room across the street to his hotel, where an immediate
change of clothes was necessary, since his suit was
damp with perspiration caused by nervous reaction
after the danger was past. Attempts were also made
to ambush him, but he fortunately escaped and kept
doggedly to his task of journeying on horseback to
hold court in different parts of his jurisdiction.

By 1870, however, the grim Ku Klux shadow always at his heels, together with consideration for the
terrific strain put upon his wife's nerves when he was
traveling about constantly menaced by these dangers,
at last induced him to think seriously of leaving the
state for a time. His life became more precious and
necessary than ever in that year too, for on November
19, 1870, his only child, a daughter, first called Lodie,
after her mother's middle name, and later Aimée, was
born; and so, despite great personal bravery, he decided that prudence made it necessary for him tempor-
arily to leave the state. The Ku Klux was dogging
him hotter than ever now, because in the summer of

1870 a strictly private letter of his had been published by Governor Holden, which had virulently attacked the Ku Klux for its various outrages on the negroes, and had cited many specific cases of its misdeeds. Hence it was that one of his August letters had the following: "I think . . . . it may be mere common prudence to get away from K. K. K. cords and daggers for a year or two. I am not going to give up my grip, but just let go to get a new hold." Another letter of the same month contains this outburst: "I wouldn't mind yellow fever, cholera, fleas, earthquakes, vertigo, smallpox, cannibalism, icebergs, sharks, or any other name or shape of horror—provided always there are no K. K. K." And this same letter, marked "confidential," has this closing passage: "Now—you go and publish this *à la Holden* and if you are not damned for it it shall not be my fault." What Tourgée particularly wished was the Consulate in South America, more particularly still in Chile, for he was fairly proficient in Spanish, partly acquired, as will be remembered, while he was a prisoner of war. He would have been satisfied had the salary been sufficient only to pay his expenses. But the position did not come; accordingly, not having found any opening that suited him, he remained where he was, still braving the dangers of the Ku Klux, even though he was *"so sick* of the whole d——d country," as another letter puts it.

The following year saw him again chasing the ever vanishing phantom of success in business. He conceived the idea that some of the timber in the state might profitably be converted into various sorts of tool-

handles, and then followed the formation of the North
Carolina Handle Company. This new firm was
started with the enthusiasm that he always showed
when he was just entering upon some new venture,
an enthusiasm that lasted to the end of his life, despite
the fact that he always failed signally in everything
that demanded business ability. In February, 1871,
he was trying to mortgage his property to obtain funds
for the new company, a practice which he always followed when in pursuit of any new financial chimera.
On February 22 he said in a letter: "I know but little
more than I did. . . . as to where the funds are coming from. . . . I am just going to trust blindly in my
usual luck and go on until I come out or am stopped
entirely." Thus, much as Robinson Crusoe hollowed
out his boat without considering how he was going to
launch it, Tourgée started in great optimism to build
the handle factory when he had no funds with which
to complete it. Further details of this affair are not
very clear, though there are still a few letters extant
showing that some business was done. Apparently it
lasted till the autumn of 1873, when the panic came.
It left him with liabilities of $30,000 and only a
quantity of unsalable stock with which to meet them;
for what little he had at this time consisted in mort-
gages on real estate. He set himself to work to pay
off these debts with his characteristic determination,
as a letter of his dated June 20, 1876, shows: "The
monetary misfortunes of which you are already informed have given me two years of very hard work,

though I can now see that they have been of great advantage to me."

It is, however, Tourgée, the successful novelist, rather than Tourgée, the unsuccessful business man, who is of chief interest; for his literary labors during these eventful years had again been resumed. At various times from 1866 to 1870 he had written articles of a political nature to some of the newspapers in his vicinity, signed "Wenckar," a variation of his mother's maiden name. Several fragments of manuscripts of his written during this period are extant, one being the outlined chapters of what was apparently to be a novel called "My Horses," full of horses and sentiment. He was a great lover of horses all his life and at various times owned some fine "steppers." Other literary relics of this period are: the concluding chapters of a novel whose events took place in Scotland, a story of "adventure and love"; fragmentary remains of a very long poem dealing with cruelty to the negro; and several speeches delivered on various memorial days in the South, filled with the usual patriotic platitudes. During 1871 and 1872, he wrote a dozen or so articles to the newspapers under the pseudonym of "God's Anynted Phue," a supposedly popular rendering of "God's Anointed Few." These articles, in the form of poems, letters and sermons, ironically attack the pride, clannishness and class hatred which Tourgée always attributed to the Southerners, "God's Anynted Phue" being a particularly crass example of Southern egotism.

But it was not until 1874 that his first major work appeared. That year saw the publication of "Toinette," which had, as a matter of fact, been written in 1868-9. Following a practice which had already been established, and which was doubtless begun as a means of avoiding personal attacks, Tourgée published this book under the *non de plume* "Henry Churton." In 1881, when the book reappeared under his own name with the new title, "A Royal Gentleman," he wrote a preface which makes plain his purpose in penning the story. He believed that the anti-slavery writers of the North had tended to magnify the chief apparent evil of slavery—cruelty to the negro—at the expense of what was the basis of the whole system, the Southern aristocratic conception of society, in which the prime element was pride of caste. With this idea in mind, he attempted to delineate types of the slave, the freeman, the "poor white," and the "royal gentleman," or the slave-holder. He wished also to show that, while slavery in name had been abolished, it was actually as much alive as ever, because the results of the Civil War had not changed, but rather strengthened, the belief of the Southerners in their superiority to the people of the North, and in their right to dominate the negro, if not physically, at least socially and politically. In other words, the Civil War had merely lopped off a few branches from the tree of slavery, but had left its roots and trunk untouched. From all this it followed, still according to Tourgée, that slavery was a much greater evil to the slave-holder than to the slave himself. These, then, were the several ideas underlying this story, which opens in 1858 and runs briefly thus:

Geoffrey Hunter, the "royal gentleman," is a typical young Southern lawyer, in whose father's house is Toinette, a beautiful slave who has only a trace of dark blood in her veins, and of whom he is very fond. He aids her in obtaining an education, with the intention of giving her her freedom, which he finally does. Meanwhile the usual result of such close intimacy follows, the Civil War comes, and Geoffrey goes to fight, leaving Toinette and their child at his home. He is severely wounded and Toinette comes to nurse him back to life and health; but when he proposes a renewal of their old intimacy, she declines unless he will marry her. This he of course angrily refuses to do, still regarding her as his chattel; she accordingly leaves him for good and they both live sorrowfully ever after.

This tale contains most of the faults and virtues which subsequently appeared in Tourgée's stories. The plot is artificial, depending largely upon coincidence; the characters, though called "types," are far from typical, because their traits are so much exaggerated. The slave, Toinette, is impossibly idealized; it is doubtful if one in a million of her class ever approached her in combined beauty, grace, intellect, and morality—for she is of course held blameless of her relations with Hunter. He is a possible figure, though he represents Tourgée's conception of the typical Southern gentleman rather than the actuality. The "poor white," Betty Certain, is also idealized far beyond her class. There are several reminders of Gothic Romance in the form of a supposed ghost, a concealed drawer, and in the attempt to create different kinds of physical horror of the midnight variety. The story is constantly interrupted by pronouncements against slavery, and eulogies of Lincoln, who is unnecessarily, not to say unhistorically, dragged in several times. And yet the tale is by no means lacking in a certain kind of merit. Impossible as the highly sentimentalized Toinette is, this first of the large family of idealized negroes portrayed by Tourgée is possibly the most impressive creation of the whole lot. Betty Certain, despite the unconvincing complexity of her character, is a striking figure at times. And in melodramatic narrative, which was always Tourgée's *forte* as a novelist, there are several really powerful specimens: Hunter's midnight search for the ghost, his rescue of his drowning son, and especially the fight between Betty Certain and Toinette's ghostly mother. All in all, however, it can justly be said that Tourgée's remark in the preface to the 1881 volume, *"it is a picture of facts,"* while not completely wrong is certainly largely so, for he here made the same error which he continued to repeat all his life: he rarely saw facts, but only their distorted images in the imperfect mirror of his strongly biased personality. The book, printed partly to help pay his debts, failed in that purpose. A letter from his publishers, Fords, Howard, and Hulbert, New York, dated July 1, 1875, states that only 2331 copies had been sold and that the loss on the edition had been about $1100. These excerpts from a letter to his wife, September 4, 1875, also corroborate the almost certain fact of the book's failure: "I fear nothing can save us from complete wreck . . . as to estate and property . . . If 'Toinette' had only been a success"—but the rest of the sentence need not be quoted.

Meanwhile his career as a judge was rapidly coming to an end, though the appellation clung to him through all his life.[1] One reform which he caused to be put into execution was the installation of heating systems in all the jails in his district; for, being much annoyed to discover that there had never been a fire in any North Carolina jail, he required a grand jury to ascertain the facts and, moved doubtless by memories of his own prison experiences, caused the remedy to be applied. The longer he was judge, the stronger became the opposition of his enemies, and in 1873 they unsuccessfully tried to secure his impeachment. On February 19 of the previous year he had tendered his resignation as a member of the board of trustees of the University of North Carolina, because the press had so severely attacked his appointment that he feared that, if he continued in that capacity, he might injure the reputation of the institution. In 1874 his friends advanced his name as a candidate for the Congressional nomination; but though he indicated his willingness to accept, in the usual "This-honor-has-been-forced-upon-

---

[1] While serving as judge, Tourgée recorded many sworn testimonials of negroes who had been the victims of Ku Klux outrages, and he later made use of many of these documents in "The Invisible Empire."

me-against-my-wishes" type of speech, the opposition was too strong and, much to his chagrin, he failed to obtain the nomination. In the following year, however, he was re-elected as a delegate to the second Constitutional Convention at Raleigh, by the largest majority ever given to a candidate from his county. This Convention strove to protect what had been accomplished by the Convention of 1868, and hence was negative in character. During this second Convention, a prominent Democrat made public threats to shoot Tourgée; but, fearless as usual, he borrowed a revolver from a friend, walked up to the man in a public place and "remained staring fixedly at him for several moments"; but no attempt was made to put the threat into execution.

In February, 1876, President Grant appointed Tourgée to the position of Pension Agent at Raleigh, and his wife was appointed clerk to administer oaths. His departure from Greensboro to Raleigh was graphically depicted by O. Henry, then a lad of fourteen living in Greensboro, who drew a cartoon entitled "Judge Tourgée Leaving Greensboro," which represents him sailing through the air on angelic wings, his left hand holding a carpet-bag, his right a handkerchief used to wipe away the tears which can be seen dropping from his one good eye.[1] So he left the place which had been a residence rather than a home for the last eleven years, but the hatred of his enemies still followed him throughout all his stay at Raleigh.

[1] "O. Henry Biography," C. Alphonso Smith, Doubleday, Page & Co., Garden City, N. Y., 1916, p. 60.

As a matter of fact, his actual home was still at Greensboro, for he spent much time at his mother-in-law's house there and bought no residence in Raleigh, but lived in a hotel; also, he retained his law office at Greensboro. In a letter written April 15, 1877, he says that the feeling against him since his appointment as Pension Agent has been stronger than ever, if possible, and that he now merely endures what he cannot avoid. He curses his folly in ever going South, and says he has stopped going to church because of persecution and vilification at the hands of supposedly Christian brethren; he bitterly attacks the South and all things Southern, and asks the friend to whom the letter was directed to be very discreet because it is "all I can do to live among these people now," and he cannot leave the South at present without serious financial loss.

In his new position, his wife did nearly all the actual work while he practised law, endeavoring by these combined means to pay off his debts. During the Presidential campaign of 1876, he made numerous speeches for the Republican candidate. Two years later he closed his law office to run for Congress in the Fifth Congressional District, and succeeded in materially reducing the majority of his Democratic opponent, but failed to be elected. He also lost much money by this venture, but was nevertheless happy in the thought that he was fighting for reform.

The closing period of Tourgée's fourteen-year residence in the South was a time of constantly increasing literary activity on his part. While still a judge at

Greensboro, he wrote two novelettes, both printed in the same volume, "John Eax" [pronounced Eex] and "Mamelon," two "rifts in the shadow" of Southern conditions, as the preface says, that almost constantly overhung him. The rift is not especially pronounced in either tale, however, for both deal largely with war conditions. The hero of "John Eax," Charles De Jeunette, of Huguenot ancestry, a lawyer by profession, marries Alice Bain, an English girl of low social rank, and thus brings upon himself the bitter hatred of his family. He is imprisoned for debt, but escapes and espouses the cause of the North in the Civil War, in which he becomes a general; and eventually, in order to inherit a large fortune left to his wife by her great-grandfather, John Eax, he assumes that name himself, this being a condition stipulated in the will. The autobiographical elements in this story are plainly evident in the hero's birth, profession and war activities, as is true of nearly all of Tourgée's novels. After the brief résumé given above, it need hardly be said that the story is almost absolutely devoid of any semblance of originality, since it has all the earmarks of the story of adventure plus sentiment which was so popular in Tourgée's day. It has the superb horses, the highly colored narrative, the impossible evolutions of character, and the attacks upon the South, so characteristic of him. The tale had its origin in a story, related to Tourgée by a good story-teller, which dealt with an old family that had once been prominent in that vicinity. On the day after he heard this story, he was unable, even amid the routine af-

fairs of a country court, to banish it with all its pos-
sibilities from his mind; and that night, from sunset
till sunrise, he wrote the one hundred and thirty-five
pages that make up the tale. Even if the physical
possibility of penning a story of one hundred and
thirty-five pages in a single night be granted, candor
still necessitates the comment that Tourgée's reputation would have suffered very little had he spent that
night sleeping the sleep of the unimaginative just.

"Mamelon" had its inception in an inscription read
on a tombstone in a neglected church-yard, whither
Tourgée wandered one day in the spring of 1874 during a lull in court affairs; and there it was that the
story thus suggested took shape in his mind, the first
chapters being written in the silence of the cemetery.
The tale is founded directly upon his already narrated
experiences with the ill-fated North Carolina Handle
Company. The hero, Paul Dewar, weds his childhood
sweetheart, Sue Moyer, and, as is to be expected, becomes a general in the Civil War. After the war,
impressed with the abundance of hickory in his locality,
the Carolinas, he starts a handle factory which lasts
until the panic of 1873. Discouraged by this disaster,
he attempts to take his own life; but the bullet, after
seriously wounding him, conveniently leaves its mark
upon a stone which he, a student of geology, has collected, together with many other relics, from an Indian
mound dubbed "Mamelon." The stone thus happily
scarred by the providential bit of lead is found to contain corundum, and the New York Corundum Company eventually becomes as successful as one wishes

that the North Carolina Handle Company might have become. The French ancestry of the hero, who, though not as usual a lawyer, is persuaded by his wife to study law, together with his final abundant success, and the features already mentioned, all combine to make a largely autobiographic and almost completely uninspired tale, which by no means implies that it does not make entertaining reading.

A letter-head found in Tourgée's personal effects witnesses that during the winter of 1875-6 he had found a new means of remuneration, in which he was ever after intermittently engaged. He gave lectures on the following topics: "The Coming Crusade"; "Today in Account with Yesterday"; "Out of the Strong-Sweetness"; "The Ben Adhemite Era"; and "Southern Humor." A copy of the "Ben Adhemite Era" only has been found, which, based on Leigh Hunt's familiar poem, paints the future in glowing colors; but it may safely be inferred from the titles that most of the other lectures dealt with the Reconstruction Period as well. This letter-head also states that the lectures were to be given by "Albion W. Tourgée, Late Judge of the Superior Court," and the "Author of 'Toinette'"; hence it appears that by this time "Henry Churton" had dropped his false garments and assumed genuine judicial robes, although as late as 1875, before revealing himself to the public, "Henry Churton" still wrote numerous articles to Southern newspapers, which attempted to show that the policy of Reconstruction was a failure.

The residence at Raleigh saw the production of

Tourgée's final literary labors completed in the South. Two were of a similar kind and were work of a technically legal nature. "The Code of Civil Procedure of North Carolina with Notes and Decisions," and "A Digest of Cited Cases in the North Carolina Reports," were both copyrighted February 9, 1878. The preface to the former volume states that the "object of this volume is to enable the professional reader more easily, quickly and certainly to ascertain what is the law in regard to practice in Civil Action and Special Pleadings." Tourgée received many letters of praise for the production of this useful book, which cost him much hard labor. It was of course written specifically for North Carolina lawyers, as was the "Digest of Cited Cases," of which there was an edition of six hundred copies which sold for twelve dollars each.

During this same year, *The North State,* a paper in Greensboro, published weekly from March 18 to May 28, and then irregularly until August 12, the "C" letters, which occasioned a really huge amount of speculation in both North and South as to their authorship and pertinence. These letters, which occupied about two large newspaper columns and always closed, "We shall see. 'C'," were distinctly journalistic in tone, being written in homely, popular style, despite frequent poetical and classical quotations. They consisted of attacks against the Ku Klux, defenses of the negro, and much satire directed against Democratic candidates for political offices, particularly the bench. The intense partisanship, inexcusable personal scurrility and mud-slinging which were everywhere present in them, together with their graphic style, caused several papers to rank them even higher than the notorious "Letters of Junius." One person especially attacked in them, Judge Fowle of Raleigh, suspected that Tourgée was the author; and, chancing to meet him one day on the streets of Raleigh, directly accused him of the authorship and followed his charge with a shower of fisticuffs, to which Tourgée promptly retaliated. He suffered more than his justly furious antagonist in this brachial contest, as his discolored countenance indicated for some time, although his epistolary accounts of this affair stoutly maintain the contrary. After this occurrence became known, it was no longer possible for "C" to hide his identity from a long curious public.

Tourgée's period of residence in the South was now nearly ended. Hatred against him had been steadily waxing stronger ever since his arrival there; and by 1879 he was satisfied that the only sensible course for him to pursue was to return to the section for which he had fought and had always defended by tongue and pen. During the summer of 1879 he spent his time in closing his business affairs, and in the month of August he and his family boarded a New York train, incidentally taking several uncompleted manuscripts, one of which, about to appear in printed form, was destined soon to make his name "known to almost every household," as a convenient expression has it.

CHAPTER III

"A FOOL'S ERRAND"

THE *New York Tribune,* September 3, 1879, devoted one and a half columns of its front page to an interview granted by Tourgée to one of its reporters on his return North. In this interview Tourgée definitely states that he had returned to a more congenial atmosphere because of Southern antagonism to all things Northern, and particularly because of its manifestations of hatred against himself. His whereabouts for the next three months are not definitely known, but it is certain that most of this time was spent in New York attending to the publication of the two books which will now be considered in detail. Although "Figs and Thistles" appeared a month and a half earlier than "A Fool's Errand," the greater historical importance of the latter work makes it advisable to discuss it first.

On October 4, 1879, the following notice appeared in the advertising pages of the *New York Tribune:* "Published This Day. Figs and Thistles. . . . Ready shortly, A Fool's Errand. Fords, Howard and Hulbert." On November 10, the *Literary Notes* department in the *Tribune* contained this item: "The advance demand for 'A Fool's Errand' has been so great that Fords, Howard and Hulbert have decided to delay the publication of it until November 15, in order to prepare a larger edition." And on that date the same paper contained another advertisement stating that "A Fool's Errand, by One of the Fools," could be purchased at all bookstores or at the publishers. The book which the public was thus anticipating, and which it has since generally regarded as the first literáry effort dealing with the Reconstruction Era; the book also which for the next few months was probably the most discussed American novel of the day; and the book which was undoubtedly Tourgée's most successful work, at any rate so far as earnings and popularity are concerned, certainly deserves considerable attention.

He himself has told how it came to be written, in a personal letter from Bordeaux, August 24, 1903. "Early on a Sunday morning in the month of July, 1877, in the city of Raleigh, . . . after a sleepless night spent in restless review of events which had occurred since the close of the war of the Rebellion, especially in regard to the relations of Northern and Southern ideas, I wakened my wife and said, 'I am going to write a book and call it "A Fool's Errand".' I immediately arose, went into an adjoining room and that day wrote three chapters of that work." This story may be continued by a passage taken from the *Personal* column of the *Tribune,* April 22, 1881, in which Tourgée is quoted thus: "I laid it [the manuscript of these three chapters] away and did not take it up again till June, 1879, when the printing began. One chapter

I wrote twenty times, and tore it down out of the type three times. Each time I threw my manuscript into the fire and entirely rewrote the chapter. I could never patch up." Apropos of the above, it may be remarked that Tourgée very frequently rewrote his different articles several times, to the constant despair of his wife, who was thus obliged to re-copy them a like number of times, and that he often wrote only in time to keep the printers busy.

So much for the actual composition of the tale. In the preface of "Hot Plowshares," May, 1883, Tourgée first discusses the serial idea that underlay the writing of six of his novels: "Many years ago the author conceived the idea that he might aid some of his fellow-countrymen and country-women to a juster comprehension of these things [Northern and Southern divergences] by a series of works which should give, in the form of fictitious narrative, the effects of these distinct and contrasted civilizations upon various types of characters and during specific periods of the great transition. Beginning their preparation in 1867, . . . he has worked patiently and honestly and zealously to complete his analysis of the representative groups of characters. . . . The period covered by the now completed series of six volumes extends from twenty years before the war until twelve years after it. . . . In chronological order they would stand as follows: 'Hot Plowshares', 'Figs and Thistles', 'A Royal Gentleman', 'A Fool's Errand', 'Bricks Without Straw', 'John Eax'." As has been true with more than one author of a series of novels, it is highly probable that this conception was by no means as clear in Tourgée's mind in 1867 as it was in 1883; for his wife, in a letter to *The Buffalo Express,* October 14, 1908, lays much emphasis upon the fact that Tourgée did not want to write any more books dealing with Southern conditions after writing "A Fool's Errand," for he feared that he would merely repeat what he had already written. His publishers, however, insisted, and he finally yielded to their importunity.

The book has its title because its hero goes through almost identically the same experiences that Tourgée himself had undergone, and comes to the conclusion which he had come to, that the attempt of the North to superimpose its type of civilization upon the South was a "fool's errand." The title was chosen also with an eye to possible pecuniary profit, for we are told that "the writer believed that the form of the title would constitute one of those pleasant literary conundrums which have a distinct market value, and would consequently enhance the sale of the book." [1] Its story is a picture of the aftermath of the Civil War in the South, and the effects upon two civilizations of that mighty upheaval. The similarity of its hero to Tourgée is even more pronounced than in any of his other books. Comfort Servosse, of French ancestry, whose family moves west near Detroit, is a college graduate and a lawyer. In the cause of the North he becomes a brigadier-general, but loses his health and hence decides to go South with his wife (Metta Ward before marriage) and small daughter, to practise law. There

[1] *Our Continent,* Vol. V, p. 604.

he is elected delegate to the Constitutional Convention
of his state, and works for the same reforms which
Tourgée had advocated in the Convention of 1868.
His life is often endangered by the Ku Klux, and he
loses the sympathy of nearly all save the negroes and
carpet-baggers.   Metta is clearly enough modeled on
Mrs. Tourgée, and the Reverend Enos Martin, Servosse's former college president, is with little doubt a
picture of M. B. Anderson, President of Rochester
University.   There is also a suspicious resemblance
between the negro, Jerry Hunt, and Mrs. Stowe's
Uncle Tom.   Tourgée often angrily denied that any
of the characters in his stories had flesh-and-blood
prototypes, but this denial is of as little value as his
constant reiteration that the chief merit of his stories
is their "honest, uncompromising truthfulness of
portraiture," as the preface to "A Fool's Errand" puts
it.   This apparent "truthfulness of portraiture" was
without doubt largely responsible for the great popularity of the book; but, like many other generalizations
avidly accepted by the public, it is founded on the
sands.

Tourgée makes much use of the Richardsonian device of letters, and constantly interrupts the really
powerful narrative with disquisitions on history, curses
loud but not always deep against the Northern policy
of Reconstruction, attacks on the South, and exuberant
praise of the negro.   These interruptions, indeed, almost spoil the story as a story, since their frequent
recurrences are so excessively irritating to the reader.
The best narrative is contained in the chapter "A Race

Against Time," in which Lily Servosse on her high-mettled steed saves her father's life from the Ku Klux, in the nick of time of course, for as usual the several crises in the tale are happily manipulated by coincidence. There is much grisly realism in the scenes where the ravages of the Ku Klux are shown. The dialogue is fairly life-like, but the story, like Tourgée's other novels, is prevailingly deficient in humor, despite, or rather because of, his conscious attempts to attain it; it was in his letters, when he was not taking himself seriously as he always does in his novels, that there is often cause for real mirth. The story contains the usual sentimental elements in the relation between Servosse's daughter, Lily, and Melville Gurney, son of a Confederate general. These young people, after surmounting the customary obstacles strewn upon the course of their true love, are happily united by the death of Servosse, an event which causes the heart of the ex-Confederate general to relinquish its hatred toward a "carpet-bagger" daughter-in-law. Yet in spite of the obvious faults which are inherent in this novel, as in others of its kind, the story really grips, as "Uncle Tom's Cabin" grips, because in each case the author had a burning message to give the world.

And it is the message of "A Fool's Errand" that is of chief importance, to which the largely artificial narrative was merely a means of attracting public attention.

On March 2, 1867, the Reconstruction Act had gone into operation, which was to be the Northern policy toward the South for the next ten years. "This famous

law consisted of two parts: five of its six sections provided for the establishment and administration of a
rigorous and comprehensive military government
throughout the ten states not yet restored to the Union;
while the remaining section, the fifth, declared that
the restoration of the states should be effected only
after reorganization, on the basis of general negro en-
franchisement and limited rebel disfranchisement." [1]
That this policy was short-sighted and fatally destruc-
tive of the very objects it sought to attain, the next ten
years amply demonstrated. Tourgée himself has indicated what its immediate effect was. "So the line
of demarcation was drawn. Upon the one side were
found only those who constituted what was termed
respectable people,—the bulk of those of the white race
who had ruled the South in the *ante bellum* days, who
had fostered slavery, and been fattened by it, who had
made it the dominant power in the nation, together
with the mass of those whose courage and capacity
had organized rebellion, and led the South in that
marvelous struggle for separation. On the other side
were the pariahs of the land, to designate the different
classes of which three words were used: 'Niggers,'
the new-enfranchised African voters; 'Scalawags,'
the native whites who were willing to accept the reconstruction measures; and 'Carpet-baggers,' all men
of Northern birth, resident in the South, who should
elect to speak or act in favor of such reconstruction"
(pp. 124-5). Tourgée had, in the Convention of 1868,

[1] "Reconstruction Political and Social," by W. A. Dunning,
p. 93.

insisted upon the following reforms which the hero of
the story also advocates: (1) Equal civil and political
rights for all men; (2) Abolition of property qualifi-
cations for voters, officers and jurors; (3) Election by
the people of *all* officers; (4) Penal reform—the
abolition of the whipping-post, the stocks and the
branding-iron, and the reduction of capital crimes
from seventeen to one or at most two; (5) A uniform
system of taxation; (6) An effective system of public
schools (p. 141). In other words, Tourgée was in
1868, before reaping the results of his "fool's errand,"
a firm believer in the Northern policy of Reconstruction. He had, as he says, "no idea that he was com-
mitting an enormity; but from that day he became an
outlaw in the land where he had hoped to have made
a home, and which he desired faithfully to serve"
(p. 141).

But bitter experience taught him the folly of thus
trying to force a proud, aristocratic people to accept a
system of government so utterly opposed to all their
traditions; and at the end of his Southern residence
he came to believe that only the enforcement of the
sixth item in the above list would produce the results
desired in the North. He first formulated this definite
educational policy, a policy to which he devoted the
larger part of his time for the next ten years or more,
at the end of "A Fool's Errand," where his mouthpiece, Servosse, states the fundamental error of the Reconstruction Act, and its remedy: "We tried to superimpose the civilization, the idea of the North, upon the
South at a moment's warning. . . . So we tried to

build up communities there which should be identical in thought, sentiment, growth, and development, with those of the North. It was A FOOL'S ERRAND" (p. 341). The remedy for this state of affairs, according to Tourgée, cannot come from within but must come from without. "The Nation nourished and protected slavery. . . . Now let the Nation undo the evil it has permitted and encouraged. Let it educate those whom it made ignorant, and protect those whom it made weak. It is not a matter of favor to the black, but of safety to the Nation. Make the spelling-book the scepter of national power. Let the Nation educate the colored man and the poor-white man *because* the Nation held them in bondage, and is responsible for their education; educate the voter *because* the Nation cannot afford that he should be ignorant" (pp. 346-7). In this book Tourgée thus merely indicates the general remedy; he was shortly to argue for the specific educational methods which he regarded as necessary to effect the results which the Reconstruction policy had failed to attain.

Scarcely had this book been given by the press to an already expectant public when the first edition was sold, and for the next year edition after edition followed in almost bi-monthly succession. The *New York Tribune* in its *Literary Notes,* December 3, 1879, makes the following comment: "Few works of the day have had a more rapid and immediate success than 'A Fool's Errand' now enjoys. No book on the shop counters sells better and the fame of it has been carried on the wings of newspapers into every State if not county in the land. Its reception in the South has not been of the most cordial kind, though the merit of it as a composition is not denied." This statement is almost literally true. Scores of Northern newspapers spoke in the most extravagant praise of the book's literary worth. Ulysses S. Grant at this time delivered a speech in which he casually made a favorable reference to "A Fool's Errand," and on the following day the firm of Fords, Howard and Hulbert was deluged with a shower of telegrams requesting copies of the book. The unknown author was heralded as the "Victor Hugo of America," and many prophecies were made that the "great American novelist" had at last arrived. *Harper's Magazine* contained perhaps the most adequate and restrained contemporary criticism. "It can scarcely be called a love story. . . . It is rather an earnest and at times passionate philippic in narrative form against the reconstruction policy. . . . The volume is one-sided, but intensely in earnest." [1] Its Northern popularity was of course not reflected in the South. A letter from the New Orleans Custom House, December 22, 1879, informed the publishers that the book was not on sale there because Southern sentiment was against it, and hence sale by subscription only was advisable. *The Raleigh Observer* grudgingly admitted that the story "is a powerfully written work, and destined, we fear, to do as much harm in the world as 'Uncle Tom's Cabin,' to which it is, indeed, a companion piece." Meanwhile speculation as to the author was rife. The *Literary Notes* in the *New York Tribune*, January 24, 1880, hazards the following guess:

[1] *Harper's Magazine,* February, 1880, p. 472.

"The list of persons to whom has been attributed the authorship of 'A Fool's Errand' grows apace. [Some of those mentioned by the *Tribune* were: the governor of South Carolina, General Ames of Mississippi, Edmund Kirk, General Joseph Abbott, Tourgée, and particularly Mrs. Stowe.] Evidently the author does not wish to be known; but those who have guessed Judge Tourgée can afford to stick to their guess." As late as August 25, 1880, the same paper says: " 'A Fool's Errand' is still selling by the thousand, and the publishers have found it convenient to make duplicate plates and print simultaneously in New York and Boston." [1]

Perhaps it will be well to see what unbiased critics at a later day thought of this book, after the tumult and shouting of contemporary criticism had died away and the story was almost forgotten. The *Bookman* speaks thus: "Of course Judge Tourgée's book was not to be compared with Mrs. Stowe's. Its subject

[1] Accounts of sales regularly sent to Tourgée by Fords, Howard and Hulbert indicate that most of the claims as to the sale of "A Fool's Errand" were exaggerated. No record has been found of the number of copies in the first edition, but by January 1, 1880, 5281 copies had been sold, including 300 in England. By June 30, 1880, 43,653 copies had been sold, and by December 31, 1880, 41,236 more. In 1881 about 9000 copies were disposed of, in 1882 about 2500, and from that time on not more than 2000 copies per year. It would thus seem that the total sale was not much more than 100,000 copies, but there appear to have been several pirated editions both in this country and in England; at any rate, Tourgée made this charge several times, and was always bitter against both national and international copyright laws. It is thus possible that the total sales of the book may have neared the 200,000 mark, for some 25,000 copies of "A Fool's Errand" were sold in the same volume with "The Invisible Empire."

made a more limited appeal; its author had no such emotional power as hers; and many chapters, especially toward the end, read like political tracts. Yet none the less, here is the most powerful and moving story of the Reconstruction period that has yet been written."[1] The *Arena* has this comment, relative to a new edition of "A Fool's Errand": "In our judgment 'A Fool's Errand' is the most valuable historical contribution to the Reconstruction period that romance literature has yet given us. . . . Aside from its historical value, 'A Fool's Errand' is a beautiful romance and an important contribution to American fiction that merits a permanent place in literature."[2] Professor C. Alphonso Smith, in his "O. Henry Biography," says: "After reading many special treatises and university dissertations on the kind of Reconstruction attempted in the South I find in 'The Fool's Errand' the wisest statement of the whole question yet made." [3]

The mystery of the authorship of the story was definitely settled in the summer of 1880 when, on May 22, "The Invisible Empire" appeared, bound in the same volume as "A Fool's Errand," with Tourgée's name on the title page as author of both works. "The Invisible Empire" aims to do about what Mrs. Stowe's "A Key to Uncle Tom's Cabin" had done; that is, present the public with authenticated records of events, which, though not precisely those narrated in the respective tales, were yet almost exact analogies. The

---

[1] *Bookman,* July, 1905, pp. 458-9.
[2] *Arena,* September, 1902, pp. 333-4.
[3] "O. Henry Biography," p. 63.

volume cites many cases of Ku Klux outrages, and
closes with an appeal emphasizing the necessity of
national education as the basis of real reconstruction.
It was printed only as a joint work with "A Fool's
Errand," and was sold only by subscription at two
dollars per volume. Over twenty thousand copies were
sold in the first half year of its existence.

As has already been mentioned, "Figs and Thistles,"
the second in the series of six Reconstruction novels,
appeared on October 4, 1879. Since it preceded the
publication of the vastly more popular "A Fool's
Errand" by less than a month and a half, it attracted
much less attention. Furthermore, it dealt not at all
with Reconstruction problems, but its events took place
wholly in the North; more particularly, the scenes of
action are mostly in Ohio, and Tourgée himself said
that in this story he paid a debt of love to his childhood
home. The period of time covered is 1850-1872.
Markham Churr, the chief figure in the tale, embodies
the usual autobiographical qualities of a Tourgée
hero: he is a college graduate, a lawyer, and a soldier
in the Union cause. Of special similitude is the wounding of Churr in the Battle of Bull Run, his consequent
confinement in a private house in Washington, his
slow recovery in his Ohio home in the spring of 1862,
and his return to the army. Eventually he attains the
rank of brigadier-general, luckily inherits a large fortune, and is sent to Congress; these were honors which
Tourgée never attained, but his heroes are always a
combination of genuine similarity to himself, plus several higher attainments of which he apparently deemed

himself amply worthy. Many critics thought that this story was intended to be a life of James A. Garfield, here concealed as Markham Churr; but this theory is rendered unlikely, not so much because Tourgée denied that it was true as because Churr is so obviously a picture of himself. Sentiment, mystery, coincidence, and absurdly impossible character somersaults appear in the customary abundance throughout the tale. The "Syllabus Personarum" in the preface makes far more entertaining reading than the story itself, which as usual is devoid of humor and contains, like most novels of its type, a sentimental sop for the public at the end, for virtue is rewarded and vice punished with the most exasperating mechanical inevitability.

During this time Tourgée was a man of affairs as well as a novelist. After the stay in New York in the autumn of 1879, where he was writing, consulting with his publishers, and doubtless very happy in the thought of the fame that would be his when "One of the Fools" should reveal himself to an expectant public, he departed to a new field. Although his bank account was rapidly swelling to a size far greater than ever previously, he had been looking about for some occupation more certain of steady financial reward than literature. After refusing an offer to enter a prominent law firm in New York, he decided to make a second migration to a far country. This time it was the swiftly expanding West that attracted him, and some time during December the Tourgée family left for Denver.

Arriving there, he at once sought an opening in his chosen profession, but none was available. An offer was at once made him, however, by the publisher of *The Denver Times* to assume the editorial management of the evening edition. Since this appeared to be fairly satisfactory, Tourgée accepted, meanwhile keeping an eye open for an opportunity to practise law. But he was not destined to remain in Denver long, either as a newspaperman or as a lawyer, for early in 1880 his publishers wrote a letter importuning him to come East and supervise a new edition of "A Fool's Errand." This he did, and again went to Denver to continue his journalistic work. But before many weeks he received a most urgent request from his publishers to write another book in the same vein as "A Fool's Errand." He at first refused to do this, because, as has already been noted, he thought it would be merely a repetition of the former book and might therefore fail. But finally he sent his publishers eight or ten chapters of "Bricks without Straw," another story that had been begun in the South. The publishers found the chapters satisfactory and he began to finish the story in Denver, but for some reason was unable to write effectively, and so started East again, probably in May, in search of inspiration. He was in Canada for a short time, hoping to feel there a mood for writing, and incidentally seeking the British copyright for the forthcoming story. By the middle of July he telegraphed his wife, requesting her to close up his business affairs in Denver and come East. Thus ended the brief Western experience, and for the next six months their home was in New York where he rapidly finished the new novel, of which the first edition of twenty-five thousand copies appeared in the first week of October, with "By the Author of A Fool's Errand" in a conspicuous place on the outside cover.

The book took its title from Exodus 5, 18: "Go therefore now, and work; for there shall no straw be given you, yet shall ye deliver the tale of bricks." In this book, fifth in point of time in the series of Reconstruction novels, "some aspects of the present condition of the colored race (1880) and their relations to the whites in the great matters of Labor and Education afford still another point of view, and present still new types of character and romantic interest," as the preface to "A Royal Gentleman" states. Despite this claim for novelty, there is really little in the book that had not already been presented in preceding tales; for Yankee school teachers, idealized negroes, and theories of national education had already characterized previous works. It does differ from "Figs and Thistles" and "A Fool's Errand," however, in that it has less of an autobiographical nature; for the hero, Hesden Le Moyne, is a Southern man with accompanying prejudices. His French ancestry is significant, however, and he had voted in favor of the new State Constitution of 1868; moreover, he is finally converted entirely to the Northern point of view, both by his wife, a New England school mistress who had become a "carpet-bagger" teacher, and by his own observations of the injustice done to the negro through the short-sighted Reconstruction policy. Furthermore, he becomes Tourgée's mouthpiece in the closing chapters, where for the first time education is not only advanced as the sovereign remedy for the solution of Reconstruction problems, but a specific method is offered to attain this end: a fund of money for educational purposes is to be distributed by the government in proportion to the illiteracy of different communities; in other words, national supervision of state schools is advocated.

In other respects, however, the story is largely a repetition of previous books, with its convenient disregard of most of the laws of probability (as evinced by several miraculous coincidences), its stirring scenes of Ku Klux Klan depredations, its element of mystery with an accompanying inept solution, its pathetically conventional romanticism, its legal and economic discussions, and its strong denunciations of Southern civilization and Northern inability to face facts. Both its strength and weakness are sufficiently pointed out in the *Dial*, which said that the Northern women who went South probably "did not as a usual thing enter on their lonely and perilous task at the childish age of seventeen; and did not invariably become at once the daring riders of glossy steeds, each endowed with the strength and speed of a locomotive, the tricks of a circus-mule, and the intelligence, docility and affectionateness of a sheep-dog. The strength of the book lies in its true-seeming portraiture of the lower order of characters; its rapid and thrillingly graphic narration of incidents both terrible and grotesque; and its tear-compelling descriptions of the sufferings of a hapless

and helpless race of beings." [1] Two weeks after the
book was placed on sale, the publishers found it necessary to make a duplicate set of plates to keep up with
the demand. Their report to Tourgée on December
31, 1880, states that 41,459 copies had already been
sold, which shows that its sale had even exceeded that
of "A Fool's Errand" for a period of similar length.

During this time, other matters than literature were
engaging Tourgée's attention. He could never resist
the temptation to engage in political strife, and opportunity was afforded him in the summer of 1880 to
take part in the presidential campaign which eventually
resulted in the election of Garfield. It so happened
that Tourgée had been acquainted with him as a boy,
for, when Tourgée was about ten years old, he had
visited some relatives in Chester, Ohio, and one of the
boarders in the family was the youthful Garfield. The
future president showed his interest in young Tourgée
by inviting him to the seminary in Chester, where the
two sang from the same song book during chapel
exercises; and some fishing trips taken together at this
time resulted in a fairly intimate boyhood friendship.
They had met again in the Civil War, and there renewed their youthful acquaintance for a short time.

On the journey East, in the summer of 1880,
Tourgée had stopped off at the Chicago Convention
and once more met Garfield, who had read and en-
joyed "A Fool's Errand," and was aware that the book
would probably have, as it actually did, a considerable
amount of influence in the campaign of 1880, by plac-

[1] *Dial,* October, 1880, pp. 110-112.

ing Reconstruction problems before the public in a popular form.[1] Hence it was not surprising that, after being nominated for the presidency, Garfield wrote Tourgée asking him to assist in the coming campaign. He eagerly accepted the invitation, and that he labored regularly at haranguing crowds in different parts of the country is shown by various speeches which still remain in manuscript form, and also by the fact that he almost entirely lost his voice shortly before the election. After Garfield had triumphed at the polls, Tourgée sent this telegram: "The family of fools send greeting." To it Garfield replied in a letter: "Dear Judge: I thank you for your kind greeting from the 'Family of Fools,' and in return express the hope that the day may come when our country will be a paradise for all such fools." Furthermore, a few weeks after his election, Garfield wrote Tourgée asking his opinion as to what effect the election would have on the "solid South," to which Tourgée replied that the result would be very good provided the Republican Party would put into effect a system of national education. In this letter Tourgée also says that even as early as 1870 he had begun to try to get the Republican Party interested in national education, and had persisted in this attempt up to the present time. In the following June, Garfield summoned Tourgée to Washington for a conference on the matter of educational

[1] "The Bystander is perhaps the only private citizen to whom a Republican President ever wrote, 'But for the publication of your work I do not think my election would have been possible.'" "A Bystander's Notes," *The Chicago Inter Ocean*, January 29, 1892.

methods. After a two hours' conversation about this matter, Garfield said: "You are right. There is no other way. We must begin—*at the beginning*. Write out your views of what is possible to be done and let me have them—or, better still, put them into a book and I will study it. Of course I must find my own way in this matter, but you can help me. No one else has studied the subject in the same way or from the same standpoint that you have occupied. . . . You must help me in this matter." [1] Tourgée promised to write the book and did so in "An Appeal to Cæsar"; but several years before it appeared, Garfield was only a memory.

Lectures, the dramatization of "A Fool's Errand," and a controversy over that book, occupied the winter of 1880-1. Tourgée spent most of this period in Philadelphia at the home of his life-long friends, both of whom he had known as a boy, Mr. and Mrs. Joseph Warner. To the list of lectures given in his Southern readings, at least two more titles were now added: "Give Us a Rest" and "How to Boss the Bosses." He usually started to read his lectures; but as he warmed to his subject, the printed pages were often thrown aside and the topic was finished extempore.

It was, however, the dramatization of "A Fool's Errand," in collaboration with Steele Mackaye, that took most of Tourgée's time during this winter and the coming summer as well. The slight success that an unauthorized dramatization had made in the West, had caused him to give notice that prosecution would

[1] "An Appeal to Cæsar," p. 17.

follow any more like attempts, and had also very probably given him the idea of making an authorized version. The business contract, drawn up between Tourgée and Mackaye on June 11, 1881, states that the plot of the play was made in unison; Tourgée wrote the first dramatic version, and Mackaye then made such changes in construction as his experience as a dramatist warranted. In matters of structure, Mackaye's judgment was final; in matters of fact regarding the South and related subjects, Tourgée's opinion was likewise unquestioned. Proceeds resulting from royalties were to be equally divided. The proceeds were, however, unfortunately very slim, for on its first appearance in Philadelphia in the end of October, 1881, the play was hissed and lasted less than two weeks. The story of the dramatic version was practically the same as that of the book, except that Servosse was still alive at the end of the play. It contained four acts of one scene each, except the third act which had three scenes, and each act closed with a "curtain thriller." Scenes of Ku Klux outrages usurped the greater part of the plot, with a corresponding lack of humor and emotional relief. The play's failure was thus about as complete as any orthodox Southerner could have wished.

Near the first of January, 1881, there appeared "A Reply to A Fool's Errand by One of the Fools," [1] written by Wm. L. Royal, a Southerner by birth, who had fought for the Confederacy and then studied law in Richmond before joining the New York Bar. The

[1] J. E. Hale & Son, 1881, New York.

géneral tone of this work is sufficiently indicated by the
following passage, taken from the preface: "I look
upon the book to which I have attempted to reply as a
willful, deliberate, and malicious libel upon a noble
and generous people. . . . I look upon its author as
one of the most contemptible fellows of those who have
libeled that people, and not at all less contemptible
because highly endowed with intellect." After paying
his respects to the cleverness and popularity of the
book, Royal bitterly castigates Tourgée for his repre-
sentation of the negro dialect, his claim that nearly all
Southern people hated the North as much as they
hated the negro, and charges him with being partner in
an affair involving financial dishonesty. The author
of this piece of mordant vituperation excelled Tourgée himself in the ability to make unqualified statements of whimsical beliefs. Tourgée replied to this
book in the *New York Tribune,* January 31, 1881, in
a four-column letter, in which he endeavored to refute
one of Royal's claims, to the effect that the chaotic state
of the South was due largely to the presence of numerous carpet-baggers. Royal then had a new edition
of his book printed, containing a "Reply" to Tourgée's
"Reply," in which a not very convincing attempt was
made to show that Tourgée had juggled figures in giving statistics, and in which also the ancient argument
was advanced that the teachings of revealed religion
show that the negro is inferior to the white. The
"Reply" closes with this Parthian shot: "Upon the
whole, I desire to say that when Mr. Tourgée under-
takes to write history, he establishes his right to the

place that his ardent admirers claim for him—to wit, that of the greatest author of fiction of the day." The *Tribune* for March 15, 1881, characterizes Royal's book by saying that the author "is satisfied with pronouncing the statements of Judge Tourgée 'as false as hell'—a mode of reasoning which can hardly be called conclusive." The book is then of little value, because the writer's prejudices were much greater than those of Tourgée; it is cited here merely because it is the chief specimen [1] of a number of attacks made upon the tenets which "A Fool's Errand" had so doughtily advanced.

Public approbation of Tourgée's literary work was shown in March of this year by a friendly dinner given him in New York by the Union League Club. The speakers who toasted him included, among others, John Jay and Joseph H. Choate. In response to their toasts, Tourgée told of an interview which he had had with President Grant, in which he [Tourgée] had suggested education as the best remedy for Southern conditions; but, having failed in his direct attempts to influence legislation, he had turned to the novel as the best means of effecting his idea of reform.

In the spring of 1881, while on a lecture trip in western New York, Tourgée saw in a Buffalo paper an advertisement offering for sale a large house and

[1] Another specimen is "Not a Fool's Errand," by Rev. J. H. Ingraham, G. W. Carleton & Co., New York, 1880, a collection of letters describing the peripatetic adventures of a Northern governess in the South. She becomes converted to the Southerners' point of view; therefore her sojourn in that region is "not a fool's errand."

some thirty-five acres of land at Mayville, New York, a village containing hardly one thousand people, the county seat of Chautauqua County, and situated on the northern end of Chautauqua Lake, only three miles from the parent Chautauqua Institution. He at once journeyed to the place, and liked it so well that before long Mrs. Tourgée was taken there for her opinion of it as a future permanent home. She was charmed with the spot, and the place was soon purchased with a part of the $60,000 which Tourgée had in the bank at that time, the proceeds of the three novels published during the last two years. The house, a fine, large mansion built and formerly owned by one member of the "Tweed Ring," needed some remodeling; but by June 1, 1881, the *Mayville Sentinel* could print this notice in the local news item: "Judge A. W. Tourgée and family are now located among the residents of Mayville, they having arrived yesterday." Tourgée made his wife a present of the place, and she at once aptly dubbed it "Thorheim."

Several reasons had influenced the Tourgées in taking up their residence in this new locality. They both loved country life, and Tourgée was inordinately fond of fishing, for which the lake, less than half a mile from his home, offered abundant opportunity. The fact that the locality was strongly Republican also appealed to him, for the taste which he had already had of public life had given him a hankering after more of it; a desire which was destined never to be very well satisfied. For the next sixteen years this place was his permanent home; and it is of course obvious that during this time "Judge Torjáy," as his neighbors called him, was the leading citizen of the sleepy little hamlet, and the recipient of many local honors. For most of the time during the next three years, however, the Tourgées were in Philadelphia engaged in a journalistic venture of no little magnitude.

CHAPTER IV

"OUR CONTINENT"

THE first number of *Our Continent,* which was published at Chestnut and Eleventh Streets, Philadelphia,
appeared February 15, 1882. This newcomer in journalistic fields was started by what was virtually a
partnership between Tourgée and Robert S. Davis;
Tourgée was general editor and Davis furnished the
major part of the necessary funds. This magazine
was, according to Tourgée, "the first serious attempt
ever made to put into a weekly the attractions and ex-
cellences of our great monthlies." [1] It proclaimed its
general purpose thus: "This journal is not, however,
intended to be the vehicle of any peculiar ideas. It
may very probably call a spade a spade, and may even
shy a brick at an especially obtrusive head now and
then, but as a rule its politics will be non-partisan as
its religion will be non-sectarian." [2] That it was prevailingly Republican in its politics, however, need
hardly be mentioned. It was indeed as large as the
average monthly periodical, and contained the usual
popular features characteristic of such productions:

[1] Vol. II, p. 477.
[2] Vol. I, p. 72.

short stories, serial stories, "Notes and Queries," "Literary Notes," "The Household," "Science," "Jottings," "Notes on Dress," "In Lighter Vein," "Home Horticulture," articles of general interest, and so forth. Thus it attempted to "lay before our readers from week to week the best thought of our best writers, illustrated by the best work of our best artists, and clothed in the most befitting garb that the highest mechanical skill can devise." [1]   The art department was managed by Donald G. Mitchell; and other writers of prominence, including Harriet Beecher Stowe, made contributions. The magazine sold for ten cents a copy and four dollars a year.

A large part of its material was of course contributed by Tourgée. Again and again in its pages he asseverated that he willingly took all responsibility for whatever appeared in it, and as usual preened himself on the fact that he was outspoken, fearless and independent. Much of his literary work consisted in the grinding of old axes: discussions of the South, innumerable defenses of the negro, and the advocacy of Republican principles, as well as attacks upon the Republican party for its failure to effect legislation leading to national education. In 1884 he strongly advocated the nomination of Robert Lincoln as Republican candidate for president, but finally acquiesced with a show of good grace in the nomination of Blaine. In addition, he wrote many articles of a purely popular nature, such as, the value of home life, proper training for rich men's sons, the necessity for all to take part in politics,

[1] Vol. I, p. 8.

warnings against the excessive use of tobacco and alcohol, attacks on the Mormons, criticisms of various authors, the part of the church in social service—and so on, in an endless variety that still had unity in the fact that these effusions were all largely cant, after the manner of most popular magazines.

One work of real importance by Tourgée first appeared in the pages of *Our Continent*. This was "Hot Plowshares," last in the series of six Reconstruction novels, though first in chronological order, for the story closes when the Civil War had just begun. This novel was started in July, 1882, and ran, with occasional lapses, until May, 1883, in the spring of which year it also appeared in book form, published, as all the others had been, by Fords, Howard and Hulbert. It was composed amid hard conditions. "This story from the first has been written under the most difficult and peculiar circumstances. It had just been commenced when it became necessary for the writer to assume the entire control and management of the *Continent,* both editorially and as a publisher." [1] Nervousness caused by summer heat acting upon his old wound and a temporary spell of eye-trouble had also hindered the composition of the tale. As the preface to the published volume states, it was "designed to give a review of the Anti-Slavery struggle by tracing its growth and the influences of the sentiment upon contrasted characters." Thus it discusses, with the usual combination of fictitious and historical elements, the growth of the Abolition movement in the North, and the Fugitive

[1] Vol. II, p. 571.

Slave Law, with its attendant, the "Underground Railroad." The main events take place in a small village in central New York.

The story gets its title from the fact that the heroine, Hilda Hargrove, is supposed to have a taint of African blood in her veins, and is therefore obliged to undergo the ordeal of public contempt; but, as might be expected, she is eventually proved to be of pure Caucasian blood, through the efficacy of concealed documents luckily found, by a crazed woman, in a secret drawer. Because of this lucky find, the "hot plowshares" Hilda "had been called upon to tread" prove harmless and she triumphantly marries the hero. He is Martin Kortright, son of the farmer, Harrison Kortright; the parent eventually becomes wealthy through the construction and successful operation of factories—doubtless another literary echo of Tourgée's experiment with the handle factory. Harrison Kortright is the best picture of Valentine Tourgée ever drawn by his son, and the conversation in the opening chapter between the Kortright father and son had actually taken place between Valentine Tourgée and his strong-willed boy. In other respects the hero resembles Tourgée only in that he is a lawyer and officer in the Union cause. The mystery of Hilda's birth furnishes the chief interest in the narrative, which is also enlivened by stirring pictures of a runaway sleigh, the destruction of the mills by fire, and the attempted abduction of Hilda. The artificialities of plot which have been noted in preceding tales appear here in wonted abundance. Repetition of the elements common to most of the five earlier novels—contrasts between the civilization of the North and the South, categorical lists of the motives which bring about certain episodes of the action, as well as eulogies of Lincoln and John Brown —abound in the story, which is perhaps the weakest in the series of Reconstruction novels, with the exception of "John Eax." The fact that it was written primarily for serial publication intensified the tendency, already strong in Tourgée, of closing many chapters with the thrill that the "to-be-continued-in-our-next" story usually strives to arouse for financial reasons.

Mrs. Tourgée's diary, May 17, 1882, reads as follows: "At Albion's request, I write that his prediction is that one year from today he will have $100,000 in the bank, outside of his property and Thorheim, and if this prediction is fulfilled, he will go to Europe and stay a year." But the prophecy was not fulfilled, for in spite of repeated assertions that *Our Continent* was a success, it soon became evident that trouble was in the air. Davis had become frightened at the possibility of failure, and transferred all his interests in the publication to Tourgée for $10,000 long before even one volume was completed.

Mrs. Tourgée worked in the office every day far more regularly than Tourgée himself, but even her great industry could by no means counterbalance the lack of business instincts in her strongly opinionated husband. By January 15, 1883, she was constrained to record in her diary this blunt fact: *"Blue day* in the office for the Judge," and this expression was often repeated in the months that followed. In July of this year Tourgée wrote to James Gordon Bennett, requesting him to help back up *Our Continent* with his capital, but no aid came from that source.

In the following October a removal was made to 23 Park Row, New York, though the Philadelphia office was retained. The change was deemed expedient because of the greater business opportunities of New York, and also because the chief persons who had offered financial assistance in Philadelphia had been a liquor dealer, an infidel, and two Democrats; it would have been gall and wormwood for Tourgée to accept aid from any of this quartet. Aid from the liquor dealer was quite certainly refused, for Tourgée would not take liquor advertisements in *Our Continent* at any price. The new situation did not, however, help matters much. Things still went from bad to worse, and by July, 1884, Tourgée's sworn statement reveals that the average monthly receipts from subscriptions were only $1425. At the beginning of this year, he used the device, so often employed by struggling periodicals, of offering prizes for the best short stories as a means of arousing the flagging public interest, as well as prizes for those who secured the greatest number of subscriptions for the magazine; and these prizes in many cases were his own novels. But all efforts to keep the publication going were vain, and on August 20, 1884, it made its final appearance. This last number, however, contained no mention of the fact that it was the magazine's swan song.

The details of its demise are not very clear, for Mrs. Tourgée stopped keeping her diary through this

troublesome period, or else destroyed it, and few authentic records have been found. But there are several
references in the diary for 1885 which show that the
latter part of 1884 was largely taken up in nerve-rack-
ing legal matters connected with the financial affairs of
the publication. It had had a capital of $150,000 com-
posed of shares of fifty dollars each, and no less a
person than Ulysses S. Grant had $1000 worth of these
shares. This is shown by his letter of July 30, 1884,
in which he asked Tourgée to return the principal and
accumulated interest, since, because of recent misfortunes, one thousand dollars now meant much to him.
Tourgée replied, stating the facts about the financial
condition of the magazine; and on October 16, Grant
answered, saying that he was unaware of these facts,
begged pardon for asking the return of the money, and
requested Tourgée not to give himself another thought
about the matter. Tourgée has briefly summed up his
experiences with *Our Continent* in this excerpt from
one of his letters: "A very rich man induced me in
1881 to engage with him in publishing the *Continent*
magazine. When his extravagance and pretense had
swamped what ought to have been a success, he dug
out and I very foolishly undertook to resuscitate the
corpse. Had I been brave enough to cut expenses
down to bed-rock, I should have succeeded. But I
was not. . . . It was a bad break—took everything and
a lot more." This was literally true, for the $60,000 re-
ceived from his books was gone, Thorheim and even
the future sale of the books themselves had been
mortgaged, and debts still remained. Tourgée went to

stay with a cousin of his in Grimsby, Canada, for some time in the autumn of 1884, trying to collect his energies to face the consequences of this most disastrous of all the blows that had thus far struck him. Meanwhile his wife remained in New York, settling the business affairs of the publication, and at the close of the year they both returned to Thorheim. This experience unquestionably made Tourgée a sadder, as well as poorer, man; but it unfortunately did not make him an appreciably wiser one.

CHAPTER V

THORHEIM

THE next twelve years of Tourgée's life (1885-1897) were spent wholly at Thorheim, save for scores of trips made all over the United States, but particularly in the eastern part, to fill lecture engagements. On the whole it was a very disheartening time, marked by steadily waning literary powers, with an accompanying diminution of sales for the products of his pen, and hence a regular lessening of income. During the last half of this period, Tourgée was little more than a hack writer, using whatever skill he had on any sort of writing that offered hopes of publication; and only too often did his manuscripts go on more than one journey only to return accompanied by the usual rejection notice, while many of them never appeared in print at all. Many articles which, after several trips to and fro, finally obtained publication, might better never have been printed so far as his reputation is concerned.

The best record of his activities during this time is contained in his wife's diary. The perusal of this fairly systematic record of his life from 1881 till his death makes it plainly evident that she was the nobler soul.

Hardly once did she fail through these years of trial and continual disappointment to be his constant inspiration; while, in a more practical sense, it was largely due to her untiring energy, despite frequent attacks of illness which often overcame her, that Tourgée's literary and business ventures attained what small success they did. Without her assistance in the office as amanuensis, proof-reader and general business manager, their financial condition would have been much worse, and the retention of Thorheim, the maintenance of which cost no little sum on account of its large size, would have been impossible. Besides this constant fear of financial ruin, she had to bear with the many irritable traits of her husband. His headstrong nature, his cocksure confidence in his own opinions, his excessive love of fishing with the accompanying waste of many valuable days, his constant desire to enter the political arena—all these well-defined traits of his taxed her wifely powers of diplomacy to the uttermost. "Blue and discouraged" recurs again and again in the diary. The following passages, selected from many of a like nature, illustrate the constant strain she was forced to undergo:

July 16, 1885. "Albion went fishing, but as usual caught nothing; but, as it does him just as much good, no one cares."

October 2, 1885. "Was glad Albion did not get the nomination." [This refers to his attempt, which had seemed possible of success, to be nominated for State Senator.]

September 30, 1886. "A serious, fruitless talk with

Albion. It is useless to hope to influence him. His own way is always the *right* way."

October 8, 1886. "Albion went this morning fishing all day and dwindled away all the golden day, when honor, which means everything, is at stake."

May 14, 1887. "Anniversary of our marriage. Still in bed and spent a very unhappy day. How the sweet dreams vanish as the years go by!"

June 2, 1887. "A rainy, gloomy day with many sad accompaniments. Albion in despair over his work. Life does not seem worth the struggle anyhow."

In spite of the despondency evident in such passages, it is nevertheless true that on the whole the Tourgées' family life, apart from financial worries, was a happy one. "So glad Albion is back," appears frequently in the diary, upon occasions when Tourgée returned from lecture engagements. The testimony of their close friends, as well as that of the diary, indicates that there was more domestic felicity at Thorheim than in the majority of households. Almost always during these years several friends or relatives shared the hospitality of Thorheim, and birthdays, marriage anniversaries, and other like times were made memorable by festive activities. When the cares of the office were off his mind, Tourgée was always excellent company, whether at the fireside or in the fishing-boat.

Tourgée's next volume, after the publication of the Reconstruction novels, was "An Appeal to Cæsar," a series of campaign documents written to influence the Republican party, symbolized as "Cæsar," to put into effective legislation his pet project—national educa-

tion. As noted previously, it was written in fulfillment
of a promise made to President Garfield, and certain
parts of it had already appeared in *Our Continent*.
It was published in the autumn of 1884, having been
dictated from a bed of pain that year. This series of
essays, written in much the same manner as a lawyer's
argument, deals with Tourgée's "FOOL'S ERRAND," to
the South and his consequent disenchantment. He attempts to show, by a long array of arguments and numerous tables of statistics, that the negro population in
the South will steadily increase, while the whites will
decrease; he discusses other plans that have been pro-
posed as a remedy for the present intolerable state of
affairs in the South and shows their inadequacy; and
he then advocates his own specific nostrum that will,
according to him, prove an infallible remedy for the
present ill, a remedy already broadly outlined in "A
Fool's Errand" and in a more detailed manner in
"Bricks without Straw," but never before treated at
such expository and argumentative length. This remedy
is national education, the funds devoted to this purpose
to be subject not at all to State control, but "to be distributed, on the basis of illiteracy, *to the various town-
ships and school-districts in which free primary schools
shall have been in active operation for a specified
period* during the time covered by the appropriation,
and having a specified average attendance" (p. 319).
He then proceeds verbally to pummel objections that
may be raised to his plan. As an inducement to the
acceptance of his scheme, he holds out the threat of a
possible future uprising of the blacks against the South

unless his method of dealing with the Reconstruction problem is employed.

Tourgée did not argue for his theory in a manner calculated to conciliate the South. "The writer knows full well that very few of the white men of the South believe that this time [when the negro receives his rights] can ever come. They think the black man's capacity for endurance has been divinely adapted to the infinity of their arrogance" (p. 404). The book closes with a final chapter urging those who read it to bombard their representatives in Congress with letters demanding that action be taken to put this educational policy into practice. Tourgée had already circulated a petition to this effect, which had been signed by some thousands of voters (p. 319).

Northern press comments on the book were as usual over-laudatory, for few of them mentioned the plainly evident conviction of infallible prophetic powers, and the usual animus against all things Southern except the negro. The New York *Nation* spoke of it thus: "We wish to do a piece of justice and frankly confess that we had a strong prejudice against Judge Tourgée as an embittered sufferer from dispelled illusions. . . . We read on with a determined intellectual resistance to the foreshadowed proposal of national interference in State affairs. But when we came to his plan of national education, we could not deny its reasonable and statesmanlike character."

This book had been written in every faith that the Republican party would triumph at the polls in November, 1884. But the election of Cleveland put a very different aspect on national affairs. As a result of this catastrophe, for such it was in his opinion, Tourgée began, in *The Chicago Inter-Ocean,* a series of weekly articles which ran from December 10, 1884, till two weeks past the time of Cleveland's inaugural in the following March. They were addressed to "A Man of Destiny," signed "Siva," and marked the beginning of a relationship with the *Inter-Ocean* that was almost unbroken for the next thirteen years. These weekly articles caused so much comment that in March, 1885, William Penn Nixon, editor of the *Inter-Ocean,* had them published in book form. The essays are political satires addressed personally to Cleveland, much like the previous "C" letters in tone, though this later work surpasses the earlier in partisan fury, rancorous invective, and nasty personalities. The following passages are the best commentary on the tone of the essays: "Knowing, as you do, how little worthy of note your life has been, and how utterly barren your mind and character are of all those elements usually accounted needful to a fit exemplification of our American life, it must be with some sense of dizziness that you find yourself about to be hoisted upon the pinnacle of national power as the representative headlight of American Statesmanship" (p. 11). "If you are a true type of American life, it is high time that we had a new ideal" (p 108). "I pity you as I do the snarling scavenger of the desert sands, because he is not fitted for better things. I pity you standing before the world as the exemplar of the American people, as I would pity a Lilliputian leper put forward as a representative and type of the unlettered giants of Brobdingnag. I pity you as an inert instrument of an unholy combination of evil purposes—the victim of a party's greed for power and of a faction's blood-stained strength. I pity you" (p. 109)—but here a stop had best be made and "pity," if not indeed a harsher feeling, be bestowed upon a man who would stoop to such indignities, upon a newspaper, partisan though it was, that would print them, and upon a portion of the public that would read and believe them. There is of course some palliation for Tourgée in that he was merely following in the steps of an innumerable host of political muck-rakers. It is perhaps better neither to justify nor condemn these ineptitudes too strongly, as well as not to take them too seriously; for the absolutely unconscious *naïveté* of the whole series of papers, in their assumption of unfailing wisdom, prophecy, and the right to act as dictatory counselor, results in giving the reader a refreshingly large amount of amusement. The question of the authorship of the papers, as in previous anonymous publications of Tourgée, was again widely discussed and many suggestions were made, including, among others, the names of Roscoe Conkling, James G. Blaine, and, impossible though it may seem, Ulysses S. Grant. By the first of August the sale of the book had netted Tourgée over four hundred dollars; but after that there was little demand for it, possibly because Cleveland's record of sturdy, uncompromising efficiency had at least partially shown how completely fatuous the chief ideas in the book had proved to be.

Still determined to nag Cleveland as much as he could, immediately after the "Man of Destiny" series had been completed, Tourgée began to bombard the Democratic administration in a new set of papers. These received the title "The Veteran and His Pipe," and ran in the *Inter-Ocean* from April to September, 1885. They consist of dialogues between several Civil War veterans, who continually praise the patriotism of the country as they knew it in their youth, and as unceasingly lament the crass indifference to country and to the heroes of the war which they see at the present time. Modern apathy to sentiment of all kinds versus old-time reverence of it, eulogies of Lincoln and Grant, vitriolic onslaughts against the Reconstruction policy, as well as against Cleveland's appointments and upon him personally because he had not fought for the Northern cause, much discussion of Southern matters already broached in Tourgée's novels, and defenses of himself from the charge that he was unduly prejudiced against the South—these are the main topics in this new series of papers, whose most noteworthy feature is an entire absence of any new ideas. They were, however, sufficiently well received by the public to justify Nixon in having them published, probably in 1886, and seventeen years later a new edition appeared.

On September 26, 1885, the *Inter-Ocean* began to publish another series of articles by Tourgée, entitled "Letters to a Mugwump," signed "Trueman Joyce," which appeared every Saturday until the middle of November. As the title implies, these letters were

addressed to the "man without a party," and advocated
that he should align himself with some definite political
organization, preferably, of course, the Republican
party. They contain hosts of truisms about the necessity of political catharsis, and allied topics. For these
articles, which averaged between two and three
columns in length, Tourgée received fifty dollars each,
and this constituted a large part of the $5500 that
was his total income for the year 1885. This income
also included some money gained from the sale of a
little property which he still had in North Carolina.
He had also some real estate in Kingsville, Ohio,
whose rental afforded him during his whole life probably about enough money to pay for the expenses in-
curred by his fishing trips. But the bills for this year
were numerous, and they, including the upkeep of
Thorheim and the interest on *Our Continent* debts,
left no surplus whatever.

Having found that his tirades against Cleveland
apparently had pleased a certain cantankerous element
in the Republican party, Tourgée began a third collection of articles that bristled with scurrilous utterances against the president in the *Inter-Ocean* on
March 4, 1886, and they ran bi-monthly until eighteen
numbers had appeared. This time the title chosen was
"A Child of Luck," and the signature was again
"Siva." The only remarkable thing in this third dia-
tribe against Democrats generally and Cleveland very
particularly, is the astonishing amount of ingenuity
displayed in saying nothing new or of any special
value in an innumerable variety of ways. There is

again evident the same debonair, patronizing, cheaply familiar, uncle-to-nephew tone that had characterized the first two series. Since these three sets of papers were entirely too innocuous to cause Cleveland to pay the least attention to them (except that he may have remarked that the "writer is probably some government Diogenes, who is afraid I will deprive him of his tub or will stand in his sunshine" [1]), there is no need to make any further comment on them. Comment might better be made on the fact that in 1886 Tourgée's lectures were going very badly, for popular interest in them was decreasing, as Mrs. Tourgée's diary plainly shows. Whereas he had usually received $100 per lecture, there is a record of one which he was now glad to deliver for thirty-five dollars; and at this time the family bills were allowed to run until they were several months overdue.

The year 1887 was marked by the publication of two more novels, in which for the first time Southern questions do not hold the place of chief interest, though echoes of them appear in the first one published, which was "Black Ice." Mrs. Tourgée's diary for January 8, 1885, states that "Albion today wrote the first installment of 'Black Ice'," and on May 16, 1887, "Sent ms. of 'Black Ice' to Fords, Howard and Hulbert," by which company it was shortly published. Tourgée needed the aid of his physician while writing this tale, as the dedication and preface show, as well as this passage from the diary, April 8, 1885: "Looked over what Albion had written of 'Black Ice' and find many

[1] "A Man of Destiny," p. 139.

alterations necessary, which it pains me to call his attention to but it must be done.'' The book was thus written in a time of great physical pain, caused largely by Tourgée's old wound and attacks of neuralgia to which he was very susceptible, and one wishes that his ill health might account for the fact that most of the weaknesses which appeared in his earlier works are found here even more prominently; but unfortunately Tourgée himself said that the story was written with the deliberate intention of justifying the theory that he held in regard to all fiction—that the only true romance is that which is built up on those rare occurrences which are the result of a series of coincidences, and that pure realism is always to be avoided, save in historical matters.

Hence the plot of this tale is even more bizarre than any of those which preceded it. The chief figure is Percival Reynolds, a middle-aged mining and civil engineer, who, with his wife and daughter, lives in a pleasant country village apparently somewhere in New York. There can be little question that the village is really a picture of Mayville; the lake, whose "black ice" gives the story its title, Chautauqua; the house, described with so much care, Thorheim; the Reynolds family, the Tourgées; the benevolent old physician, the family doctor to whom the book is dedicated, Dr. William Chace; and the span of horses, those that Tourgée was taking so much pride in at that time. Furthermore, the reader is told that two of the characters in the novel were married at Columbus, Ohio, on May 14, by the Reverend Julius E. Gardner,

which is precisely autobiographical. The first few
chapters present a really pleasant picture of domestic
tranquillity in the small village, and one only desires
that Tourgée might have written the whole book thus;
but, true to his theory, he soon converts what might
have been a rather charming picture of village life into
a hodge-podge of mystery, suspense, fortuitous com-
binations of events, horror, and crime. The titles of
several chapters will sufficiently point out the general
structure of the tale: "The Breaking of the Seal";
"Some Raveled Threads"; "The End of the Chase";
"A Midnight Horror"; and "In the Pale Moonlight."
The following passage, taken from the chapter called
"A Midnight Horror," shows how well Tourgée had
mastered the art of conventional melodrama:

"My heart was in my throat as I peered forward at
the roadway with unnecessary care. A rustle in the
hemlocks by the roadside startled me as if it had been
a thing of terror. I pulled the reins and stopped the
surprised horses at the very steepest part of the
declivity. As I did so a shriek, clear and shrill, rang
out of the unseen space beyond, and echoed and re-
echoed across the river.

" 'My God!' I exclaimed, 'that is a cry for help!'

"The cry was repeated, shriller, clearer, and un-
mistakably in a woman's voice."

This passage illustrates why Tourgée's novels were
fairly successful with the public; and very likely another reason for this success was the justification, dwelt
upon particularly in this story, of coincidence as opposed to the regularity of nature. " 'Such things are

"happening" every day. Some call them the result of chance. . . . I may be a fool, but such things, which seem against Nature, are to me conclusive evidence of One that uses and controls Nature. Call it what you will, I love to call it God'" (p. 405). The modern reader, however, is much more likely to designate this theory of his by some such unmetaphysical term as a lack of constructive ability, or even sheer mental laziness.

The second book, which had appeared from the press of Roberts Brothers, Boston; about the first of September, was begun November 22, 1886, and was called "Button's Inn." In writing this tale Tourgée was particularly interested in Mormonism, which he had previously attacked in *Our Continent;* but he was here more concerned in tracing its origin and the philosophy of its evolution from the religious life of the time. So it happens that "Button's Inn" contains about as many disquisitions on religion as Tourgée's earlier stories had contained chapters on history and social theories. This story, even more definitely than the preceding one, has its scenes in the vicinity of Thorheim. "Button's Inn," so named for its owner, had once been a real inn, standing some five or six miles northwest of Mayville on Portage Road—a name given because it was first used by the French and Indians as the route by which their goods were carried between lakes Chautauqua and Erie, the particular points of connection being Mayville, Westfield, and Barcelona, once a flourishing harbor, now merely a moribund hamlet marked chiefly by some dilapidated fishermen's huts and a ramshackle hotel. As in "Black Ice," the pastoral part of the story is rather pleasant; but one learns in the very first chapter that the inn is haunted, and from that point on the story becomes a blend of love scenes, suspense, crime, and discussions of Mormonism. The events take place mostly on Christmas Eve and Day, 1842, but part of the tale is concerned with blood-curdling incidents that happened eighteen years earlier. The inn-keeper's son, Jack Button, is a wild young fellow in his youth, who finally commits a murder in self-defense and for love, and hence is forced to flee. He becomes a convert to Mormonism, and finally returns to his old home, where he is unknown until he reveals himself. He is the real "hero" of the tale, though the more conventional one (that is, the one who marries the inevitable pretty girl) is Ozro Evans, son of the woman for love of whom Jack Button committed murder. Along with the pretty girl, there is bestowed upon Ozro the scarcely less inevitable fortune, inherited through his father's will, which he increases by means of a combination of inventive genius and business ability. The story is almost wholly a refutation of the prefatory statement that accompanies it: "My purpose has been faithfully to depict the life which marked the period," and instead represents merely another of the countless hosts of marriages that have taken place in fiction between sentimentality (in this case both of love and religion) and Gothic Romance. In this tale, as is usual in Tourgée's novels, the ghost turns out to be one of substantial flesh and blood, which has carried on its nocturnal activities by means of a trap door.

The inventive genius of Ozro Evans may possibly be an embodiment of an unsuppressed desire on the part of Tourgée to win recognition at the patent office. During a large part of his life, he spent many hours working on mechanical devices of much variety. Hundreds of dollars were spent in these efforts, dollars which would have done far better service had they been applied to some of his long-standing debts. When he was in the South, he had tried his brain and hands on some of the machinery of his handle factory, and from that time on he never entirely left off such endeavors. Some of his projects were, the making of an all-steel harness for horses, iron posts, and new brands of wrenches. He obtained one patent at least, in January, 1889, for an hydraulic motor, but it did not prove to be of any financial value. Even while Consul at Bordeaux, he still kept on with various schemes of this sort.

During the following year (1888) two more books were published, in the first of which Tourgée returned to the South for inspiration. This was "Eighty-Nine," or "The Grand Master's Story," which appeared in April. The author's name is given as Edgar Henry, and Tourgée tries to make anonymity doubly strong by having Henry state that he is merely editing his friend's life from an "original manuscript." This friend is Royal Owen, a Georgian, who resembles the usual Tourgée hero in his Huguenot descent, his farmer parent, his study of law, and his love of speedy horses. While the book in general is only a repetition of oft-repeated theories about the South and contains the usual historical and hortatory chapters, Tourgée adds two new ideas, for one of which he was plainly enough indebted to the Ku Klux Klan organization. This is the "Order of the Southern Cross," which Owen originates in obedience to the dying injunctions of his father that he should help the South in every possible way. This order advocates "peaceful revolution" rather than the actively hostile methods of the Ku Kluxers. Its members are pledged not to take up arms, but by legal means to prevent negroes from attaining inordinate political power. It is a secret society and its members wear white clothes as a disguise—both Ku Klux ideas. The hero is thus Tourgée's conception of the ideal Southern man. Not much is said of national education, but its remedial powers are implied, and Cleveland is again sharply attacked for his failure to put such a policy into law. Tourgée's private correspondence shows that the book was also intended to be a surreptitious attack on the Standard Oil Company, because of its monopolistic practices, and this explains the anonymity of the story. One of the characters in the tale has lost all his possessions and his reputation because he opposed the activities of the "Rock Oil Company," which is only another name for the company actually existing. The purpose of the book, then, was two-fold: it aimed to show that, while at present "the South was in the saddle and monopoly in the stirrup," as a poster advertising its appearance stated, the South could be ejected from this saddle by means of the "Order of the Southern Cross," and that monopoly could be forced out of the stirrup by the use of impartial legal justice. The title was intended to indicate what benefit the year 1889 would bestow upon the United States, if, before that time, these two methods of reform were employed.

The other book, which probably appeared in July, was "Letters to a King," most of which had already been published piecemeal in various religious papers. The volume is very similar to "Letters to a Mugwump," except that the mugwump is here treated more respectfully by being honored with a regal title. The letters have the twofold aim of pointing out to the "king" (who of course symbolizes the American youth who has recently come to voting age) that he has a great responsibility, and that he must accordingly be intelligent in order to meet its demands. This means, as one might surmise, that these letters gave Tourgée another chance to indulge in that form of writing in which he was so expert—the production of a chain of age-worn truisms, which rolled unceasingly from his affably condescending and unconsciously tiresome pen.

Thus far Tourgée had written only sporadic series of articles for the *Inter-Ocean;* but, beginning in May, 1888, he wrote regular weekly contributions for that paper under the caption "A Bystander's Notes," and continued to do so with practically no omissions until August, 1893. These articles, signed by his own name, constituted an enlarged "Migna," the department in *Our Continent* in which he had discussed all sorts of political and social questions in a popular manner. "Waving the bloody shirt," education, labor and capital, foreign affairs, book reviews, the World's Fair, attacks on the Democrats, alternate defenses of the Republican party and mild assaults on certain of its policies which were opposed to his ideas—such subjects as these were discussed by him in "A Bystander's Notes" many, many times. In 1889 he used a new heading, "A Tidewatcher's Thoughts," for part of that year, in which he "studied the tide of today's life." More and more these articles became propagandistic in tone. In October, 1891, he made a public appeal in the "Notes" for the formation of a "Citizens' Equal Rights Association," which was of course intended for the special benefit of the negro. He formed this organization because, as one of his letters of this period states, he had come to feel that it was impossible to influence the North by merely writing and speaking for the negro, and had therefore decided to employ more business-like means. Tourgée received hundreds of letters, mostly from negroes, praising him for this idea, and so started the association on its way; but, like his other various schemes, it soon ended in failure. The publishers of the *Inter-Ocean* found it necessary several times to refuse articles of his which attacked certain Republican principles with undue vigor, because the paper depended for its success upon political patronage. Tourgée also wrote articles for this publication on noteworthy occasions, as, for example, on the deaths of Henry Ward Beecher and John A. Logan, the latter of whom he extolled to the extent of ten thousand words. Had all these *Inter-Ocean* articles appeared in book form they would have made some eight or ten fat volumes; but this material would have been even more ephemeral than much in his actually published books.

"With Gauge and Swallow, Attorneys," which came from the press in 1889, had already been published by Lippincotts.[1] This book, as the preface states, was written to show how much romance there is in the supposedly matter-of-fact legal profession; it is thus a sort of sequel to "Black Ice," in which, it will be recalled, the theory was advanced that all life consists of romance governed by caprice. It is composed of thirteen short tales, each complete in itself, but all having the same hero, Gerald de Fontaine, a farmer's son, who had begun the study of law as a clerk, but who eventually attains eminence in the profession itself. The "romance" which is the basis of each story is composed of the customary blend of highly improbable concurrences, technical legal matter, thrilling crises, sentimentality, and prescience on the part of certain individuals, the whole resulting in patent artificiality. There are several negroes in the tales, but no specific discussion of Reconstruction problems.

For 1890 several events in Tourgée's life are worthy of note. He was summoned to Washington in March to address the House Committee on Education, which he did on the thirteenth of that month. In his address he opposed the Blair Educational Bill which was then before Congress, and advocated one of his own con-

[1] *Lippincott's Monthly Magazine,* Philadelphia, vols. 40-44, inc.

coction, which formulated the same ideas that had already appeared in "An Appeal to Cæsar." On the twentieth of March he had the satisfaction of seeing, from a place in the gallery, the defeat of the Blair bill, while on the following day he appeared before the Committee on Elections and spoke in favor of a bill then pending, which was intended to protect the voter without regard to race or color. In April he was granted a pension of six dollars a month, including the years from 1863 (in which he had renounced his pension from patriotic motives) until 1890, and thirty dollars a month for the rest of his life. On June 6, according to his wife's diary, he "covered himself with honor" by delivering a fiery address on the wrongs done the negro before the First Mohonk Negro Conference in Ulster County, New York. During this summer, in his *Inter-Ocean* articles, he advised that the Afro-American League, an organization fairly active at that time, should be a secret affair in order that it might escape persecution in the South; and for this advice he was roundly attacked by scores of newspapers.

"First bound copies of 'Pactolus' received," says Mrs. Tourgée's diary for March 27, 1890. This is a reference to "Pactolus Prime," a book on which Tourgée had been busy for over a year. "I do not know what it will do, but it is a very strong book, or else I am a very silly man," he says, in a letter about it. In this story he made use of the popular interest in the Blair bill by writing a tale in which this bill was attacked, and his old "Appeal to Cæsar" remedy again recommended. The title of the book is the hero's name, and he is a mulatto who, in order to save his children (in whom no trace of negro blood appears) from the stigma of their birth, hides from them the fact that he is their father, and takes a position as boot-black at a Washington hotel. Tourgée, as usual idealizing the negro almost to the point of apotheosis, endows Pactolus with the argumentative ability and technical knowledge of a lawyer, and with an uncanny prescience of men and affairs. The gentle reader is asked to believe that even men high in the nation's councils "were not ashamed to consider his warnings" (p. 25). Melodrama and mystery often meet together in this novel, while gushing sentiment and religious piety frequently and fervently kiss each other. Pactolus, from being an unbeliever in the "white Christ" who "exists for whites only," finally accepts Christianity with an ardor fiery enough to suit even the idolizers of E. P. Roe—with whom, incidentally, Tourgée was always on friendly terms. It is quite possible that Tourgée may have got from Roe hints of the device, so frequently used by that perpetrator of several viciously virtuous pieces of fiction, of hurling many souls into the hopper of atheism, whence they finally emerge, after a severe jostling and grinding process, as uniformly orthodox Victorian Christians. The publishers' preface to the book refers to Pactolus as "the Edipus of American fiction"; but this particular "Edipus," instead of tearing out his eyes as a self-punishment, suffers the ignoble fate of being mortally injured by a runaway horse.

Mrs. Tourgée's diary for September 17, 1889, records this item: "After a year and a half of thought, Albion began today his story. The agony—I can use no other word—of decision was intense. He wished to do so well—to put so forcibly the truths which have weighed upon him so long." This refers to a story first called "Nazirema, or The Church of the Golden Lilies." Under that title it had appeared in *The Advance,* a humanitarian weekly journal.[1] In November or December, 1890, Fords, Howard and Hulbert printed it under the new title "Murvale Eastman, Christian Socialist." The Kingsleyean title indicates the general nature of the book, which is a plea for the application of the principles of Christianity to modern industrial problems. This doctrine is embodied in the person of Murvale Eastman, a "muscular Christian," pastor of the Church of the Golden Lilies, who is of course a paragon of "body, mind, and spirit" perfection. He literally practices what he preaches by acting as driver of a horse-car, by which means he pays his own expenses and gets in touch with life as well. Finally he forms a "League of Christian Socialists," which formulates feasible methods of putting into practice the theory of the golden rule. There is a reminder of Tourgée's early literary experiments in the form of a minister named "God's Anynted Phue," who is the same type of person that he had been when Tourgée used his name in North Carolina. Secrecy, sentiment and crime add their customary zest to the tale and, in spite of their absurdity, serve to make readable

[1] *The Advance,* Chicago, vol. XXXII.

what would otherwise be a dry, theological tract. Eastman succeeds in converting enough people to his socialistic conception of Christianity to satisfy even the most egregious demands of those who insist upon religious conversions as a necessary concomitant of every good novel, somewhat as the healthier-minded Elizabethans liked those plays best which ended in a general slaughter of the leading characters. The villain of the story, Wilton Kishu, richest member in Eastman's congregation, after indulging in the usual amount of emotional acrobatics, is thoroughly cleansed of his former nefariousness and becomes a humble worshipper of the victorious Eastman. Even the substantial quantity of flesh-and-blood mystery, crime and sentiment which composes the narrative part of the book is not sufficient to conceal the very evident skeleton of propaganda which constitutes its framework. One of the members of the firm that published the story objected strongly, in a letter to Mrs. Tourgée, to the "elaborate disquisitions, which in my opinion clog the current of the thought as much as the possible current of the sales." This criticism proved to be prophetic, for the book was by no means a financial success.

In the spring of 1891, Tourgée, who had been appointed Honorary Professor of Legal Ethics in the Buffalo Law School at the time of its foundation in 1887, and had already delivered lectures there during the last four years, gave a course of lectures at that institution on legal ethics. Since Buffalo was only some sixty miles from Thorheim, he found it easy to make the journey to and fro without staying in the city over night. He held this position until he went to France, and the income thus derived was especially welcome during these years, for the sale of his books was now steadily approaching the vanishing point.

The *Inter-Ocean,* in July, 1891, began a series of articles by Tourgée, entitled "John Workman's Notions," which were popular presentations of topics concerned with contemporary political economy. John Workman professes to be a great friend of the laboring classes. He discusses the historical background of his subject, and then applies the lessons drawn from this study to modern conditions. There can be little doubt that Tourgée was mainly indebted to Ruskin for most of his ideas on political economy, for he reaches much the same conclusions as Ruskin had reached twenty years earlier, and advocates many of the same fantastic remedies which the great Victorian had already suggested. All these articles, forty-four in number, were written particularly with the intention of giving the poor nobler ideas of labor. Tourgée expected to publish this series in book form, and even copyrighted a forthcoming volume; but it never was printed, probably because he decided that the unsatisfactory sale of his previous works of a similar nature did not warrant any hope that a new volume would meet with any better financial success.

Tourgée went to California on the first day of April, 1892, and stayed there until the eighth of May, in order to recuperate from a combination of ills—the ever troublesome spinal wound, nervousness, and general physical and mental depression. Hardly had he returned, much refreshed, from this brief respite from almost unceasing labor, when he called down scathing denunciation upon himself because of a prophecy that he had made in an *Inter-Ocean* article to the effect that, unless different governmental methods were used, there would be an uprising of the negroes within the next ten years that would equal if not exceed the French Revolution in terror and bloodshed. Both the Northern and Southern press joined in vigorous condemnation of this new Tourgée jeremiad, but he insisted that the prophecy would come true and used the columns of the *Inter-Ocean* for defending himself in his usual intrepid fashion. As late as 1903, in a letter to Nixon, he still maintained that such an uprising, accompanied with terrible slaughter, was almost inevitable.

In "A Son of Old Harry," published in 1892, Tourgée employed some methods of modern realistic fiction which he affected so frequently to despise. The story was written to show that no one can escape from an evil destiny if fate has so ordained it. Yet, while the doctrine of fatalism is the foundation of the tale, it contains little compelling power; for Tourgée, in the use of coincidence, not only goes beyond Thomas Hardy, but also comes very near giving the story a conventionally happy conclusion, which would be irritating if it were not so patently impossible. In other respects the novel is characteristic of the Tourgée *genre:* horses and horse-racing are even more in evidence than in any of his other tales; the hero, Hubert

Goodwin, becomes a brigadier-general in the Civil War; there is much discussion of religious matters; melodrama plays its wonted inevitable part; and sentimentality oozes from almost every page, appearing in an "eternal triangle" in this story—a type of emotional debauchery, it should thankfully be noted, in which Tourgée seldom rioted. The racial problem is broached several times, but not to excess. The whole book presents a pathetic picture of a mind that was in nearly all respects Victorian, floundering in the effort to make literary capital of some elementary theories taken from the gospel of realism; a mind that, after giving up this vain attempt, returns with manifest relief to the comfortably familiar regions of grotesquely impossible romance.

The Chicago World's Fair called forth Tourgée's next volume, written with deliberate intent to make money out of that international event. "Out of the Sunset Sea," which appeared early in 1893, recounts in the first person the adventures of an Englishman, Arthur Lake, who, after divers exciting experiences in both love and war, embarks with Columbus on his voyage of discovery, and later succumbs to the lust for gold that seized so many adventurers at that time. This, Tourgée's only experiment in historical romance outside of his own country, is in some respects his most successful book. He himself thought that it contained his best writing, and there are good grounds for agreeing with this opinion. First of all, it is not a novel of purpose, and hence is primarily a story, one that abounds in active and swift narration, with no pauses for pointing the morals that blemish rather than adorn most of his tales. Furthermore, his other faults are less in evidence here : there is less melodrama than is customary, sentiment is kept well under control, and piety is fortunately almost completely absent. The characters are of course perfectly conventional, the hero being the ordinary swash-buckler so common in stories of adventure; but after all, in a novel of this kind characterization is of secondary importance. An almost complete absence of that constant straining for effect which is so noticeable in his other stories, results in the presence of something that is almost, if not quite, charm. In general there is nothing of originality in the story, but Tourgée in it did fairly well what many have done poorly and only a few excellently. The conversation of the sailors, however, is of a sort that certainly never was on land, though possibly it may have been on sea. One reason why the story is told better than usual is that the plot was here made almost ready to hand; for it was in the structure of his plots that Tourgée was generally weakest, weaker even than in character drawing. Another reason is that the subject furnished all the romance necessary without the necessity of painfully seeking it. The volume was popularized by drawings made by his daughter, Aimée, who also illustrated several of his other works.

One of the books so decorated was "An Outing with the Queen of Hearts," which appeared in 1894, and is a pleasant pastoral sketch. The "Queen" is Mrs. Tourgée, whose unfailing counsel and assistance merited a greater reward than this small volume gave.

But, small as the book is, it shows how deep and abiding was the affection of husband and wife, despite the temporary vexations that depressing financial troubles occasionally caused. This story, as well as "Out of the Sunset Sea," has some real charm; a charm that is, however, often distinctly impaired by bitterly one-sided attacks on modern ideas of love. But the glimpses of quiet, undisturbed nature, of fishing and exploring, slight as they are, nevertheless will probably remain with the reader long after both the plots and characters of some of Tourgée's more pretentious literary efforts have vanished from the mind.

From this time until the spring of 1895, there is little known about Tourgée that is of interest. "A By-stander's Notes" had been discontinued by the *Inter-Ocean* in August, 1893, and this suspension caused worry that was not alleviated until Tourgée was allowed, some four months later, to resume the series. In January, 1894, a second series of articles on "A Man of Destiny," once more by "Siva," was begun and continued weekly till the following April. This new production was such in name only, for nothing novel was added in this last flamboyant fulmination against Cleveland. At the end of this year, Tourgée's activities with the *Inter-Ocean* were ended until he went to France, from which place he occasionally sent his ideas. His long and fairly regular connection with this paper was certainly his most successful financial enterprise, for it was the only one that had given him a fairly steady income. Visions of political office

again haunted him in 1894, and several papers in his
vicinity advocated his election to Congress; but he
was opposed by most of the organs even of his own
party, though one had the temerity to suggest his name
as vice-presidential candidate for 1896. But the slight
sentiment in favor of his nomination to Congress soon
died an even swifter natural death than is ordinary in
politics, and with its decease all of Tourgée's hopes for
popular approval of his political theories flickered out
forever.

Still unwilling to learn, or more probably incapable,
harsh though the word is, of learning from the stern
teachings of experience, in the spring of 1895 Tourgée
started another journalistic venture in that optimistic
frame of mind which he always displayed when beginning to chase the *ignis fatuus* of business success.
On March 20, there appeared from rooms at 457
Washington Street, Buffalo, *The Basis; A Journal of
Citizenship,* edited by Tourgée. Its front page proclaimed its modest mission to the world in flaring type.
That mission was to be "The Basis of Public Peace,
Personal Security, Equal Right, Justice to All, Good
Laws, Good Government, National Prosperity, Im-
proved Conditions, AND OF A BETTER WORLD
TOMORROW." The first editorial states that *The
Basis* is a "thirty-two page weekly which hopes to
grow to forty-eight pages and then to sixty-four if
the favor of the public will permit." The general idea
of the publication, as announced, was to promote "applied Christianity," the theory which had already
been advanced in "Murvale Eastman"; but it is very

plain that a scarcely secondary purpose was to furnish a medium for "A Bystander's Notes" and various other articles of Tourgée's, together with several by his daughter, who signed herself "Henry Churton Jr.," which had been rejected by certain magazines. "Migna," which had been sleeping in a corner of the grave where *Our Continent* had rested for eleven years, was now exhumed and at least partially revivified. The history of that unfortunate magazine now began to be repeated, and the next year was painfully employed in disheartening efforts to make *The Basis* succeed, attempts that were hindered by almost constant ill-health. As early as July, Tourgée's private correspondence shows that the magazine was likely to stop at any time because of insufficient funds. Efforts to merge it with several other publications had failed, since the editors were too wary. Tourgée stated that he himself, his wife, daughter, and one office girl did the whole of the work for the magazine, which had only eight hundred subscribers. By December it had become necessary to limit the publication to once a month, and in April, 1896, the last number came forth.

The rest of this year was spent in the attempt to obtain publication for articles which almost always were rejected, but two small volumes finally found their way into print. The first of these, "The War of the Standards," is a study in "coin and credit versus coin without credit"; in other words, it is a series of campaign documents. They are largely historical, but those at the end discuss certain concrete methods of dealing with the currency problem that was the chief issue in the campaign of 1896. Possibly of more interest, because it is fiction, is "The Mortgage on the Hip-Roof House." It is a novelette of the Horatio Alger type, in which there are a villain, a poor but lovable grandfather, a more lovable granddaughter, an adopted grandson (adopted of course that he may wed the granddaughter), and a kindly as well as rich benefactor. The plot centers about the necessity of raising a mortgage on the family home, which is situated near Lake Erie. Needless to say, it is raised, villainy is properly punished, and poverty-stricken, spotless virtue is amply recompensed for its unswerving adherence to the straight and narrow path.

Tourgée went to New York in the autumn of 1896, and remained there for several months seeking publishers for various articles, as well as an opportunity to campaign for McKinley. His letters to his wife during this period often threatened suicide unless he found some means of sustenance. At last this was obtained through campaign speeches made for the Republicans, and thus the tension caused by a really desperate financial situation was relieved. After such experiences as these, it is no cause for wonder that, on December 31, Mrs. Tourgée exclaimed, in the privacy of her diary: "The close of the most distressful year of my life! Pray God the next may be different!"

Fortunately it was, for in 1897 Tourgée was appointed Consul at Bordeaux. In January he began to send letters to the President as well as to various men in Congress in regard to a consulship at Manchester. He received some encouragement in this attempt, because of which Mrs. Tourgée went to Washington in April and had many personal conferences with those in authority. As a result of these conferences, Bordeaux was finally chosen, since it was the most available position. On May 6, President McKinley informed Mrs. Tourgée that the appointment to Bordeaux was settled, and one week later the commission as Consul to that place was granted her husband. The next six weeks were occupied in settling up business affairs, and on July 3 Tourgée took what was to be his final look at his native country, and, accompanied by his wife, sailed for France.

CHAPTER VI

BORDEAUX

AFTER a stop at Gibraltar, Tourgée landed on the southern coast of France, arrived at Bordeaux on July 22, and took formal charge of his office on August 2. The duties incumbent upon him were not arduous, and, had his health been good, there would have been much happiness in store for him and his family, for the daughter came to Bordeaux shortly after her parents. But the next eight years was a time of steadily declining vigor for Tourgée, broken by periods of apparently returning strength; not only his old wounds, but a complication resulting from them which took the form of diabetes, became gradually more malignant. And yet it was not on the whole an unhappy period, at least in comparison to the preceding six or eight years, for his income was now definite and regular.

In 1898 his old publishers, Fords, Howard and Hulbert, brought out a volume of three stories, of which the first furnished the title, "The Man Who Outlived Himself." In the caption story, Tourgée again shows that interest in things supernatural which had already been manifested in some of his writings. The leading figure in the story purports to have been one of the inmates at Libby prison when Tourgée was there, and he entrusts the "strange story" of his life to his old fellow-prisoner. The tale, which contains occasional gruesome touches and uncanny situations that suggest Poe, recounts how one Arthur Quitman died while in the midst of financial troubles, came back to life, and finally recovered his memory, together with his wife and daughter—much of which is suggestive of autobiography. The second story, "Poor Joel Pike," is reminiscent of Tourgée's lawyer days. Joel Pike is a Pactolus Prime-like figure who suffers under the suspicion of being a villain, whereas he is eventually shown to be almost an angel—albeit a very ugly one—in disguise. Autobiography, mystery, problems of Reconstruction, love, and a dark, scheming villain who is finally reformed, equally spoil the closing story in the volume, "The Grave of Tante Angelique."

In September of this year, Tourgée's connection with the *Inter-Ocean,* to which he had made regular contributions since coming to France, particularly patriotic articles dealing with the Spanish-American War, was finally severed. Three months later the family took up residence for the winter at the Villa Trocadero, a pretty spot on the seacoast about fifty miles from Bordeaux, whither Tourgée went because in it were medical baths which had been prescribed for him. The family remained there until April, 1899, when, upon their return to Bordeaux, a disagreeable incident occurred. On the twelfth of that month, a bailiff, with a writ of *saisie-gagerie* issued by local authorities, entered Tourgée's house and, after handling him and his daughter roughly, took an inventory of the furniture and made insulting remarks about the American flag. This action raised the question of the inviolability of consular material, sustained by treaty, and accordingly Tourgée immediately sent all the facts to the mayor of Bordeaux and to Washington. After a good deal of diplomatic correspondence, the matter was satisfactorily adjusted.

During the coming summer and until well on in 1900, Tourgée's health was apparently the best it had been for several years, as a result of which he resumed writing, mostly about political matters, for several magazines. For the next two years his health was still such that he was able to do a little literary work at various times. One item is of much interest in view of the fact that it shows how absolutely at this time Tourgée had given up all the educational theories which had been the foundation of the Reconstruction novels and of much of his other writings. In a letter to President Roosevelt, on October 21, 1901, Tourgée first congratulates him for the moral courage shown in his invitation to Booker T. Washington to dine with him, and then says, apropos of the question of national education as a remedy for the negro problem:

"It was a genuine fool's notion. I sincerely believed at that time (1880) that education and Christianity were infallible solvents of all the evils which have resulted from the white man's claim of individual superiority. . . . Today I am ashamed to have been that sort of a fool. I realize now that . . . education does not eradicate prejudice, but intensifies it—Christianity does not condemn or prevent injustice done to the weak by the strong, but encourages and excuses it."

This letter is clear proof that the rosy visions about humanity's betterment which Tourgée had so long entertained had now entirely faded. The peevish, Timon-of-Athens tone (attributable in part perhaps to Tourgée's state of health) here manifested is obviously enough that which is usually assumed by most would-be alleviators of human ills, when their theories, based upon the insecure foundations of prejudice, sentiment, and the self-satisfaction derived from blind adherence to their own plan to the exclusion of all others, have been finally proved false by the beneficent corrosion of time.

In this same year was published what was probably the last literary effort of much length undertaken by Tourgée, and it is an only too painful evidence that his fountain of inspiration had not only ceased to spurt but almost even to bubble. In the *National Tribune,* Washington, D. C., there appeared weekly during March and April, 1901, successive chapters of a novel-ette, "The Summerdale Brabble." The action begins in Summerdale, Massachusetts, but soon switches to Tourgée's old home at Mayville, and local scenery thence plays a large part in the story. Hero and heroine are both even more extraordinary for wealth, good looks, and general personal attainments than had been customary in Tourgée's works. The only thing which prevents the tale from being an almost perfect example of consistently impeccable dulness in plot, character types, and action, is that it contains no real reprobate who has the blood-curdling attributes of all orthodox bad people.

The current of life ran smoothly for Tourgée in 1902, but the next year brought renewed troubles for both body and mind. On June 25, 1903, he received a message from Washington inquiring whether he would like a position as Consul-General at Halifax. He at once replied, stating that he much preferred to remain at his present post; but several weeks later an official announcement came that he had been appointed Consul-General at the newly suggested post. Though deeply hurt at what he regarded as a personal rebuff, he replied in a quiet letter, maintaining that he could not go to Halifax because the rigorous climate there would probably be disastrous both to him and his weak daughter. In response, he was told that if he preferred he could go to Prague or the West Indies, but that his successor at Bordeaux had already been appointed. This last communication alarmed Mrs. Tourgée so much that she dared not show it to her husband, but instead wrote a pleading letter to President Roosevelt. Having waited in vain for a reply, she sailed on July 25 for the United States, determined to have a personal interview with the President. No sooner had she landed in New York than she received a cablegram stating that Tourgée was to be permitted to remain at Bordeaux "because of Madam's letter to the President." [1] But this affair had a most disquieting effect upon her husband, for, in his wife's own

[1] *The Buffalo Express,* December 12, 1909.

words, he "never recovered from the shock of this experience, and though he lived nearly two years after, he was never again his bright, hopeful self." [1] The active cause for this episode was that certain dealers in hides in Bordeaux thought that Tourgée was too strict in his regulations concerning exportations, and accordingly made complaints to the authorities. It should be noted that Tourgée was never in his life in Halifax, though several abbreviated biographies of him state that he was Consul-General there during the last years of his life.

Meanwhile his health was steadily declining, though at times he appeared almost well; and from this period on his wife did practically all the business connected with his office. A letter of his, dated November 23, 1904, gives his own estimate of his condition: "My health was very bad for several months [1904], but in August last the doctors made an excavation in my hip and took out a piece of lead which must have been wandering around in my anatomy since Perryville. I have been much better since. I now weigh 175 and feel almost well, except for my hands which are painfully hypersensitive—making writing a burden which has so long been a delight." This letter shows that unwarranted hope of recovery which so often characterizes persons whose course is almost run. Uric acid poison was now filling Tourgée's system, and he also frequently experienced choking spells caused by water on the lungs which had to be drawn off several times. On December 30, 1904, Mrs. Tourgée said in her diary,

[1] *Ibid.*

"Began reports which may be for the last time." She of course knew that the end could not be far off. During the spring of 1905, Tourgée was dilirious much of the time, and often thought that he was dying, though he still sat up as late as April 25.

Mrs. Tourgée's diary, which had so faithfully narrated the events of her husband's life for more than twenty-five years, on May 21, 1905, recorded the closing scene thus: "The sun shines brightly, but it is a dark day for us. Albion breathed his last at 12:15 this morning. My heart is wrung. I can say no more." Two days later funeral services were held in the English church at Bordeaux, and the body was immediately taken to a crematory at Paris. Mrs. Tourgée and her daughter spent the next few months in settling up the business affairs of the Consulate office, and in November returned to Thorheim, bringing with them the ashes of the husband and father, which were shortly interred in the local cemetery after appropriate ceremonies had been conducted by the Grand Army of the Republic. A simple granite shaft was soon erected over the ashes, which bears the inscription:

"I pray thee then
Write me as one that loves his fellow-men."

In personal appearance, Tourgée was of medium height, and, while a young man, was very slim, as a photograph taken when he was in the army witnesses.[1] As he grew older, he increased considerably in weight and breadth, and during the last ten or fifteen years

[1] "The Story of a Thousand," p. 209.

of his life was quite obese—a result not only of age but of disease as well. His hair was very dark brown and he wore a heavy moustache; his face was perhaps strong rather than handsome, though he was possibly better looking than the average man. He unequivocally liked at least one custom of the Southerners—their style of dress, which he always followed after his return North, particularly as regards the wide-brimmed hat for which the "Southern colonel" on our stage has always been conspicuous.

CHAPTER VII

CONCLUSION

A CONTINUALLY lapsing interest in his novels with their already antiquated or largely discredited theories, and an unbroken absence of eight years from his native land before his death took place, account for the fact that there was little critical comment about Tourgée or his literary work after his decease. The penalty of faint praise or decorous silence thus inflicted upon him was that which is usually paid by men of his type: opportunists, who make literary capital out of some tremendous social convulsion whose surgings are soon calmed by legislative measures, or simply by the progress of time with its accompanying increase of more charitable, because less interested, opinions; politicians, whose acrid partisanship, which stains not merely their political views but also their opinions on nearly all those public and private questions which admit of manifold interpretations and solutions, almost completely ostracises them from fellowship with those who believe that one of the chief glories of literature is the possibility it affords for a comity of infinitely varied ideas; writers, whose literary style depends for its effectiveness largely upon the persistent use of devices long since hoary with age. And by this time it should be evident that Tourgée's works come, with almost unbroken regularity, under this three-fold classification: they give vent to narrow, cramped ideas; they are the products of particular, and therefore temporary, social conditions; they lack stylistic distinction.

One subject but little touched upon thus far concerns Tourgée's opinions about some of the chief writers of his day. His views of his contemporaries are to be found mostly in *Our Continent,* but he occasionally interpolated them in his novels. It was of course a maxim of his literary as well as political faith to admire only those writers whose minds ran in much the same channels as his own. This means, in general, that the Victorians were the objects of his adulation. Particularly did he reverence them for the chief article in their creed: the interpretation of everything terrestrial by what they conceived to be celestial standards. That idea which permeates so many of their writings, "And the Lord spake unto Moses, saying"—whatever any particular Victorian Moses thought the Lord commanded him to write for the betterment of humanity, to Tourgée's mind constituted their greatest charm. Thus in an article on Reade and Trollope he says: "He [Reade] recognized the underlying truth of all artistic production, that its highest purpose is to teach a noble lesson." [1] In another article,

[1] *Our Continent,* Vol. V, pp. 634-5.

entitled "The King is Dead!" he praises Longfellow in these words: "He was easily the first of American poets." He "won his crown by Americanizing the world's life. . . . As compared with England's poet laureate he was perhaps less rich in fervid imagery, but he was of deeper and tenderer tone, of broader and riper manhood, closer akin to the great common heart and less tainted with any narrow and bigoted exclusiveness." [1] The same article contains much more perfervid praise of Longfellow's Americanism. Tourgée, indeed, thought that American literature was destined to surpass that of the Old World, as is evinced by an article called "Americanism in Literature," in which there are these passages: "The American element in literature is simply the American element in our thought. . . . The coming American novelists may choose to portray the universal humanity only in Old World phases, but they will view such foreign life from a standpoint peculiarly their own, and will give new interpretations to characters and events which the Old World has but. dimly understood and only half appreciated." [2] E. P. Roe was the beneficiary of a special amount of laudation. "Few men have extended a healthier influence upon the life of today than Mr. Roe. In these times, when the novel of purpose is made a matter of artistic ridicule by our over-refined dilettanti, and the novel without a purpose is corrupting the heart and brain of the rising generation . . . the very large sales which

[1] *Our Continent*, Vol. I, p. 178.
[2] *Ibid.*, Vol. IV, p. 219.

his works have had disclose to us the pleasing fact
that our American reading public is not yet entirely
given over to the worship of the realism which insists
that fiction shall be given up to the painting life as it
is, dirt and all." [1]   Tourgée further elaborates his
belief in the purpose novel in these words: "A novel
without a purpose is the counterpart of a man without
a purpose.   One written for mere amusement may be
either good or bad, but at the very best, is only the low-
est form of art." Self-defense was probably the motive
which prompted the above words.   Dickens, George
Eliot, Ruskin, and other lesser figures often received a
word of commendation from Tourgée; in the case of
George Eliot, he failed to grasp the significance of her
minute searchings for environmental causes as the
motivations of good and evil actions.

Against everything that savored of realism in modern fiction, and against all writers who did not tread
the path of indisputable morality, Tourgée was relent-
lessly hostile.   His novels abound with references to
these matters.   "Black Ice" (pp. 18-19) : "They [mod-
ern realists] tell us that fiction is of necessity limited by
its sterile commonplaces to laborious self-dissection
and elaborated display of the results of morbid mental
anatomy . . . I had come to think that if the life
which is portrayed in our so-called 'realistic fiction' is
a fair average product of our institutions, the time
cannot be far distant when the killing of an American
will be no more counted homicide than the drowning

[1] *Our Continent,* Vol. III, p. 669.

of supernumerary puppies." [1] "Button's Inn" closes
with this querulous sentence: "We . . . assert that pettiness alone is truth and declare that real life is concerned only with multitudinous trivialities, discover-
able only by elaborate processes of morbid self-dissection." "Murvale Eastman" (p. 113): "So, too, the
pessimistic philosophy which calls itself 'realism' in
art and literature, always is, and always will be, at
fault when it comes to solve the riddle of humanity.
It says human nature, human character, is a result of
the operations of natural laws. So it is; but those laws
are not all physical, nor purely mental. The soul must
be taken into account if we would comprehend humanity or truly portray character." Again in the same
book (p. 165): "You see, the 'realist' is always ready
to believe anything mean; but anything decent and
manly he declares at once to be unnatural." Also
(p. 214): "It is only romantic notions of love and
virtue that we fear today; and these we seek to fore-
stall by prescribing for the young soul the carefully
elaborated daily record of the world's infamies, and
substituting 'realistic' impurity as a motive for 'healthy
fiction,' instead of the silly sentimentalism of old-
fashioned love." "An Outing with the Queen of
Hearts," (pp. 49-50): "I suppose we should yet speak
of it [sex attraction] as love, and go on believing in
it to the very last, had not 'realism' and the curious
contempt for all things American, which has come to
lift us up to the sublime level of social formalism by
which the society of other lands is shaped into such

[1] *Our Continent,* Vol. III, p. 732.

matchless excellence, taught us that belief in love, and
more especially in married love, is not merely the very
'worst possible form,' but a vain and weak credulity
in which only 'the immature American' is any longer
willing to admit himself so foolish as to indulge."
Again (p. 64) : "The man who paints warts and weakness, sin and shame, may tell the truth; but it is an
insignificant truth, unworthy of the artist's skill, unless
it bring some lesson of cause or cure."

Tourgée's works do not lack specific references to
some of the chief exponents of these modern ideas, or
of many other ideas that would not bear the lynx-
eyed scrutiny of such believers in strictly orthodox
virtue as himself. In an article which attacks Emer-
son for his irreverence, there occurs this sentence : "A
disciple of Carlyle, he regarded man as chiefly created
that he and his master might scold and scourge him,
though unlike Carlyle he believed in and expected his
improvement." [1] Tourgée abominated Carlyle; he
praises Auerbach because he was a lover of humanity,
and hence just the opposite of the "blustering scold," [2]
Carlyle. In "Murvale Eastman" (p. 415) we are told
that Carlyle is "the cowardliest of braggarts with his
dog's heart and envenomed tongue"; while in the same
book (p. 454) we learn that the chief impression which
Tourgée obtained from reading the "French Revolution" was of "the froth of Carlyle's rabid ravings."
Also, Tourgée praises Froude's biography of Carlyle

[1] *Our Continent*, Vol. I, p. 242.
[2] *Ibid.*, Vol. I, p. 120.

because, as he says, it is just that a "man who assumed
to denounce and scourge others"[1] ought not to have
his own shortcomings treated with lenity.   Feelings
of professional jealousy undoubtedly had something to
do with Tourgée's frequent snubbing of Howells and
James, though he was occasionally constrained to give
both some grudging praise.   Howells is a "merciless
satirist of Boston life, who paints its pettiness and self-
sufficiency so deftly that his victims take his ridicule
for praise—that universal pessimist" ("Letters to a
King," p. 71).   And while he admits that "no modern
novelist has more grace and vigor or finer sense of
literary form"[2] than Howells, Tourgée also speaks of
him as "pouring forth page after page of inconceivable
agony over trifles too insignificant for ordinary mortals
to note. . . . A picture is not truthful merely because
it has dirt in it. The province of true art is to portray
the meaner phases of nature only as a foil for the
nobler and grander passions."[3]   The last sentence is of
great significance, for it succinctly states Tourgée's
abiding conception of the function of literature.   The
chief fault in the works of Howells and James is, according to Tourgée, that the soul has been left out.[4] He
positively abhorred Hardy. Of his "Two in a Tower"
he says: "Never was more hideousness conveyed in
a simple story— . . . The realism of Zola is sufficiently atrocious, but it is not reductive. . . . —for

[1] *Our Continent*, Vol. III, p. 698-9.
[2] *Ibid.*, Vol. IV, p. 733.
[3] *Ibid.*, Vol. IV, p. 252.
[4] *Ibid.*, Vol. I, p. 796.

cool sensualism, expressed in decorous ingenuousness, combined with ignorance of what woman really is, in soul, feeling and purpose, commend us to 'Two in a Tower'." [1] As an amusing contrast to these onslaughts on three of the greatest novelists of the time, Tourgée's effusive admiration for a now almost forgotten lady novelist may be cited: "Miss Rhoda Broughton has won for herself a peculiar place among modern novelists. She has had her admirers by the hundred thousand, and her critics in equal numbers, but of imitators she thus far has had none that are worth considering. Her originality of style, indeed, renders imitation well nigh impossible." [2]

It was against Russian fiction, however, that Tourgée aimed his heaviest verbal artillery. Of Turgenev he does indeed admit that his "pen-pictures of lower Russian life were the first step toward the redemption and elevation of the Russian people"; [3] but he is unable to find language scorching enough to express his contumely for Tolstoi, particularly because of his theories about love. These stabbing words may be found in "An Outing with the Queen of Hearts" (p. 43): "We are even told that love is no secure foundation for happiness in married life, which should, instead, be based on 'mutual esteem and forbearance.' Indeed, one of the chief priests of this newfangled doctrine of life-relations has gone so far as to declare that marriage itself is 'the most sinful form of love,'

[1] *Our Continent*, Vol. III, p. 732-3.
[2] *Ibid.*, Vol. III, p. 91.
[3] *Ibid.*, Vol. IV, p. 411.

which itself, so he assures us, is of the devil and altogether vile. I thank God that he is not an American." And in "Murvale Eastman" (p. 214) we are advised that "a generation to whose lips the pessimistic foulness of Tolstoi and his imitators has been commended as an inspiring cordial, not only by the high priests of literature, but by ministers of God, is perhaps beyond fear of peril from the highly-spiced narratives of social peccadilloes which abound in the daily press." One can scarcely refrain from wondering whether the strongest superlatives in our tongue would have enabled Tourgée to express even a tithe of his disgust could he have read, let us say, "Ann Veronica"!

Toward science Tourgée was more charitable than toward realistic literature. He looked upon it at best, however, as of secondary importance in comparison with the value of the emotions, and was frankly suspicious of some of its hypotheses. In "The Apostle of Evolution," [1] he praises Darwin for his love of nature and sweet-tempered endurance of adverse criticism, but is non-committal in respect to the theory of evolution, which he regarded of value chiefly because he thought it helped to substantiate his theory of moral progress. In "Murvale Eastman" (p. 266) he says: "Evolution is the law of attribute, whether it is of species or not. . . . The dead hand of an ancestor reaches often across even a century and grips us by the heartstrings. God has consecrated this law to human progress." And again (p. 274): "Science has taught even the most incredulous of saints, within the

[1] *Our Continent,* Vol. I, p. 226.

life-time of many now living, to admit what was before esteemed blasphemous, not merely as a fact, but as a beautiful and harmonious revelation; so that we read to-day the record of God's work in veritable tables of stones which his hand has traced and his wisdom preserved for our instruction and delight." But it was exceptions from the law of regularity that most arrested and fascinated his ever-credulous mind. A passage from "A Son of Old Harry" (p. 92) will substantiate this: "The student of heredity in the human family is ever and anon confounded with seeming miracles. . . . . In spite of the principle that like produces like, we meet every day with instances of unlikeness so startling as to confound the observer, and, for a time at least, destroy all faith in scientific theories of life." Tourgée's belief in the inviolability of the exceptional, of the miraculous (in a word, of the romantic), was much stronger than his belief in the inviolability of the laws of heredity and environment. Ironically enough, it so happens that his own life is a rather unusually good illustration of the workings of those same laws.

Much in Tourgée's novels and in nearly all his other work is of interest not so much to the student of literature as of politics. His devotion to his particular party, as well as his unconcealed disdain for the opposing political faction—a disdain that only too often expressed itself in numerous screeds which lacked dignity, fairness, impersonality and breadth of view, and showed, in their stead, far too much pettiness, superficiality, pettifoggery, and feebly sardonic humor

—are quite characteristic of the political sound and fury of his day. The paper for which he wrote, *The Chicago Inter-Ocean,* was one of the chief sinners of the time against public good taste, and not a few of Tourgée's splenetic articles contributed to the sum total of its sins—sins which were probably the main cause for causing its loss of patronage, and eventual absorption by another paper. What it lacked in political fairmindedness and foresight, it endeavored to atone for by strident animosities and jaundiced flapdoodle; qualities which Tourgée, both because of his temperament and training, commonly found very pleasing to his own conception of partisanship.

"My poor husband! How his life was embittered, ruined, by his trying to do what he had no capacity to do!" Thus Mrs. Tourgée laments, as usual with acuteness of perception, the chief reason for her husband's failure to win greater success than was granted him. Multiplicity of interests was perhaps the main cause why he never attained lasting peace of mind. Had he been content to devote himself only to writing, his life would have been freed from that continual strain of slaving for the necessities of existence which he was subjected to during his last twenty years— but no, this would not do; instead, he must, despite the pleading admonitions of friends and relatives, invest the neat fortune he had won from several of his most successful books in a hazardous journalistic experiment, which resulted in a smash that ruined his financial prospects forever. He must capitalize his literary talent; and the result was mutually self-destructive, for both money and mental peace were gone. From this time on, he was forced to engage in an unbroken struggle to find a market for his various literary efforts, in order to keep his family in moderately good circumstances; and hardly was this goal reached by means of his appointment as Consul than failing health ensued to cloud the last eight years of his life. "I would have been a much better writer and far greater novelist had I been content to do less pretentious work," Tourgée says in one of his last letters; and had he said "less diffuse work," the self-criticism would have been still more pertinent.

"Somehow I have never thought much about fame and really do not know that I would care to forego today's dinner for tomorrow's praise. . . . Yet I believe I have the true artistic instinct. The idea of carving out a grand presence, a noble character—of impressing and at the same time bettering humanity—is so strong with me that I find myself absolutely absorbed by it." Thus runs a passage from one of Tourgée's letters to his daughter, for whom he always coveted greater rewards than were ever granted him; rewards that, probably impossible of attainment by her because of insufficient artistic and literary ability, were made forever unattainable by an early death. His remark about fame should be largely discounted, for he was afflicted with as much of the "last infirmity" as are most literary men; whenever "critic peep or cynic bark" touched his works either because of their extreme ideas or artistic faults, and pointed out how they had few permanent literary qualities, he was always ready to leap valiantly to their defense. While at work on any of his novels, he was almost completely absorbed in his task—except when the lure of the rod overcame him. "There is no happiness for me except in doing—achieving. If I cannot accomplish, I prefer not to be," he says in another letter, in which he also significantly states that he cares little for music, but likes plays because they present the multitudinous activities of life; a fact, among others, which witnesses that his was a nature deficient, on the whole, in the appreciation of delicately refining humanistic values. He had too much love for applied ethics to be much interested in strictly eclectic mental and emotional pursuits. Not art for art's sake, but art for morality's sake, was what spurred his mind to activity; and such a conception of the function of literature peremptorily excluded finesse from his writings. Serenity, poise, austerity, disinterestedness, catholicity,—of such enduring literary values he was almost destitute; instead, he exemplified that love for applying a quality of virtue by no means always unstrained to specific and concrete problems of the day, which, despite its frequent abuse of art for didactic uses, is one of the perennial glories of English literature.

This last consideration may well lead to a final estimate of Tourgée's place in that literature. Generally speaking, his works suffer, as most Victorian literature suffers, because of their dual aim—artistic excellence plus doctrinal inculcation. More particularly, he stands out as the author of one purpose novel that, principally because of its timeliness, took the country by storm. The burden of that novel he later expressed in this passage taken from a poem of his, which, like the other comparatively few rhymes that he fashioned, has all the vigor of his prose:

> "Yet up from the Southland comes a moan
> Like Yesterday's ceaseless monotone.
> Hark! 'Tis the half-freed Slave's lament.
> For the bliss we promised and woe we sent!
> The moan of the fettered, untaught soul
> Charged with a freeman's power and dole!" [1]

His literary work which preceded "A Fool's Errand" never attained popular success, though "Toinette" is with little doubt the first piece of fiction dealing directly with the problem of Reconstruction; for the non-partisan tales of Constance Fenimore Woolson which, first published in magazines in the seventies and eventually appearing in book form as "Rodman the Keeper" in 1880, showed the utter depression, the yet unquenched bitterness, and the pride, still splendid in desolation, of the South, postdated the appearance of "Toinette" at least a year. But "Toinette," pioneer in a literary land though it is, and worthy in many respects of comparison with Tourgée's better known writings, never caught the popular fancy —perhaps because it was a pioneer. After the extraordinary success of "A Fool's Errand," Tourgée began to experience the misfortune that second or third-rate genius must always suffer; he had burnt up al-

[1] *Our Continent*, Vol. I, p. 329.

most all the enthusiasm he had in this first great, consuming effort, and spent most of his remaining life in a vain attempt to revive the ashes. Or, to change the figure, he summarily exhausted his one narrow vein of literary ore in "A Fool's Errand" (or, more generally, in the six Reconstruction novels), and occupied the rest of his days largely in working and re-working the barren material that was still left in this vein. Continually failing in this attempt, he was at the same time forced to eke out his decreasing income with efforts to strike a paying vein in some new literary mine, which efforts usually proved to be worthless. The first mine was amply large, for it contained the endless ramifications of Southern Romance, whence, during the eighties, much valuable ore was exhumed by several writers of greater ability than Tourgée; but unfortunately, in this many-branched field, he saw only the single vein of partisan interpretation of the Southern mind and character. The reading public, however, soon tired of his "political documents";[1] not because they were documents only, for they were more than that, but because they were pervasively political, and represented an attitude that both unimpassioned, judicial criticism and popular interest could not long tolerate.

Judgment of a writer like Tourgée, as of much greater writers (Dickens, for instance) whose faults are unusually patent, is always likely to err on the side of harshness. There is, to be sure, little possibility

[1] "A History of American Literature Since 1870," by Fred Lewis Pattee, Century Co., New York, 1915, p. 318.

that the uniform edition of his works which he so much wanted to see published will ever appear. Public concern in the particularly relevant problems of his day has since been largely shifted to more immediate matters; his point of view was too individual, hence too restricted, to cause any notable imitations of the works, though he was unquestionably instrumental in stimulating much Northern interest in the South. He neither followed nor started any very distinct literary tradition; rather, he spent his strength in an attempt to alleviate a social ill which could not be cured by any such ineffectual palliative as the bigotry which results from clannish instincts, lack of well-balanced judgment, myopic political vision, and a sense of personal wrongs. Never did the spectator's attitude toward life attract him; he was not interested in the enchantment which the flux of things has afforded to some rare and precious writers; he was interested in the things themselves, and in only a restricted portion of them at that. To be in the world, yet not of it, was not for him. He hated with perfect hatred anything that savored of dandyism or of a dilettante attitude toward life, and attacked it with unrelenting acerbity. There was no neutrality for Tourgée; a belief, a political policy, an institution, must be either cold or hot, else it received from his pen a doom similar to that which was meted out to the church at Laodicea; and he often doomed it anyhow because, even though unneutral, it was too cold or too hot. And yet out of such qualities as these comes his chief virtue: he exemplified in his writings the magnificent, whether credible or not, folk-lore tradition that, in this universe of good and evil, of light and darkness, of justice and injustice, of love and hate, of God and the Devil, the positive quality of good is not only destined to win an eventual victory over the negative quality of evil in a future world, but that it often wins it here and now. Hence heroism almost invariably sweeps on to triumphant victory in Tourgée's novels, while villainy is punished with no less regular uniformity, as is demanded by the *mores* out of which come the ideas of popular literature. It was his misfortune that his particular interpretation of these eternally opposed principles did not happen to be adequate for the settlement of the questions of Reconstruction, especially in regard to the black race. Settlement of this special matter is still problematic, while the general question has now become worldwide; and the words concerning Comfort Servosse, with which Tourgée concluded the next but last chapter of his greatest novel, may now, with but slight textual change, be aptly applied to himself: "Time smiles grimly as he traces anew the unsolved problem which mocked the Fool's heart."

BIBLIOGRAPHY OF TOURGÉE'S PUBLISHED WRITINGS, AND PERIODICALS EDITED BY HIM

1867 *The Union Register,* weekly newspaper. Greensboro, January 3-June 14.

1868 "The Code of Civil Procedure, to Special Pleadings." Prepared by Victor C. Barringer, Will B. Rodman, Albion W. Tourgée, Commissioners of the Code. Raleigh.

1874 "Toinette: a Novel." New York. [New edition, 1875; revised edition, 1879.]

1878 "The Code of Civil Procedure of North Carolina with Notes and Decisions." Raleigh.

1879 "A Digest of Cited Cases in the North Carolina Reports." Raleigh.

"Figs and Thistles. A Western Story." New York. [New edition, 1883.]

"A Fool's Errand, by One of the Fools." New York. [Printings: November (2), December (2); 1880, January, February, March, April, May (2), June (2), August (2), September, October, November (2), December (4). New edition with "The Invisible Empire," 1880, 1883, 1902.]

1880 "The Invisible Empire." New York.
    "Bricks without Straw." New York. [Several
        reprints on unknown dates.]
1881 "A Royal Gentleman" ["Toinette" renamed]
        and "Zouri's Christmas." New York. [Sec-
        ond edition, 1884.]
    "Aaron's Rod in Politics." *N. A. Review,*
        February, pp. 139-162.
    "Reform versus Reformation." *N. A. Review,*
        April, pp. 305-319.
    "The Christian Citizen." *The Chautauquan,*
        November, pp. 86-91.
1882 "John Eax and Mamelon, or The South without
        the Shadow." New York.
    Our Continent, weekly magazine, Philadelphia,
        New York, February 15, 1882-August 20,
        1884.
1883 "Hot Plowshares." New York. [*Our Conti-
        nent,* July, 1882-May, 1883.]
1884 "An Appeal to Cæsar." New York.
1885 "A Man of Destiny." Chicago. [*Inter-Ocean,*
        December, 1884-March, 1885.]
    "Letters to a Mugwump." *Inter-Ocean,* Septem-
        ber-November.
1886 "The Veteran and His Pipe." Chicago. [New
        edition, 1903. *Inter-Ocean,* April-September.]
    "A Child of Luck." *Inter-Ocean,* March-No-
        vember.
    "Study in Civilization." *N. A. Review,* Septem-
        ber, pp. 246-261.

1887 "Black Ice."   New York.
     "Button's Inn."   Boston.   [New edition, 1897.
     Chautauquan Book Store, 1908.]
     "The Renaissance of Nationalism."   *N. A. Review,* January, p. 1-11.
1888 "Eighty Nine."   ["89"]   New York.
     "Letters to a King."   Cincinnati.
     "A Bystander's Notes."   *Inter-Ocean,* May,
     1888 (with occasional lapses) to January,
     1895; August, 1897-September, 1898.
     "The South as a Field for Fiction."   *Forum,*
     December, pp. 404-413.
1889 New uniform edition of: "Black Ice," "Bricks
     without Straw," "Figs and Thistles," "A
     Fool's Errand," "Hot Plowshares," "John
     Eax," "A Royal Gentleman."   New York.
     "With Gauge and Swallow, Attorneys."   Philadelphia.   [*Lippincott's Monthly Magazine,*
     December, 1887-August, 1889.]
     "Shall White Minorities Rule?"   *Forum,* April
     pp. 143-155.
1890 "Pactolus Prime."   New York.
     "Murvale Eastman, Christian Socialist."   New
     York.   [New edition, 1892.   *The Advance,*
     Chicago, vol. XXXII.]
     "The Right to Vote."   *Forum,* March, pp. 78-92.
1891 "John Workman's Notions."   *Inter-Ocean,* July-
     May, 1892.
1892 "A Son of Old Harry."   New York.

1893 "Out of the Sunset Sea." New York.

"The Anti-Trust Campaign." *N. A. Review,*
July, pp. 30-40.

1894 "An Outing with the Queen of Hearts." New
York. [*Cosmopolitan,* November, 1891, pp.
70-84.]

"A Man of Destiny." [Second series.] *Inter-
Ocean,* January-April.

1895 *The Basis.* Weekly, March-December; monthly,
December-April, 1896. Buffalo.

1896 "The Story of a Thousand." Buffalo. [*Cosmopolitan* (in part), November, 1894-April,
1895; completed in *The Basis.*]

"The War of the Standards." New York.

"The Mortgage on the Hip-Roof House."
Cincinnati.

"The Reversal of Malthus." *Am. Jr. of
Sociology,* July, pp. 13-24.

"An Astral Partner." *The Green Bag,* July-
August.

"Some Advice to Young Voters." *The Golden
Rule,* October 1, pp. 4-5.

1898 "The Man Who Outlived Himself." New
York.

1899 "A Quiet Corner in Europe." *Independent,*
June 1, pp. 1483-1485.

"The Twentieth Century Peace-Makers." *Con-
temp. Review,* London, June, pp. 886-908.

1901 "The Summerdale Brabble." *The National
Tribune,* Washington, March-April.

1902 "Our Consular System."   *Independent,* January
        23, pp. 208-210.

Two foreign translations of "A Fool's Errand" have
been found: "Eines Narren Narrenstreich," by E.
Pennet, Berlin, 1882, 3 vols.; "Hullum Hritys," by
Waldemar Churberg, Helsingissa, 1883, 2 vols.

INDEX